ROBERT MAXWELL as I Knew Him

Other books by Eleanor Berry, formerly known as Eleanor Beckman:-

Tell us a Sick One, Jakey

Never Alone with Rex Malone
(a ribald ambitious black comedy, a story powerfully told.)
(*The Daily Mail*)

"I was absolutely flabbergasted when I read it." *Robert Maxwell.*

The Ruin of Jessie Cavendish
(Miss Berry is to literature what Hieronymous Bosch is to Art) -
International Continental Review.

Your Father Died on the Gallows
(A unique display of black humour which somehow fails to depress
the reader). *The Rugby Gazette.*

ROBERT MAXWELL
as I Knew Him

A Black Comedy

Eleanor Berry

MERLIN BOOKS LTD
Braunton Devon

For my brother Nicky who introduced me to Robert Maxwell.

British Library Cataloguing in Publication Data

Berry, Eleanor
Robert Maxwell as I Knew Him
I. Title
338.761070172092

ISBN 0–86303–653–8
Printed in England by The Basingstoke Press

It was the late sixties. A hulk of a man, who looked like a beautiful big black labrador, was easing his Rolls down the Mall in the direction of Buck House.

He approached the roundabout where Queen Victoria, her face stern and her hand touching the royal orb, peered down upon him.

The car phone rang.

'So then, Mr Maxwell, what are you doing about your overdraft?' The caller's voice lacked the simpering whine which invariably infuriated Robert Maxwell. It was loud, confident and strident as if its owner was uninhibited and incapable of fear.

'Who the hell are you?' asked Bob, mildly irritated but impressed at the same time by the caller's boldness.

'Nicholas Berry. Financial Correspondent of the *Daily Telegraph*.'

'Would you care to come and see me this evening for a drink, Mr Berry? I'll hand it to you that I like your journalistic style.'

The study in which Bob met my brother Nicky for the first time was dark, sombre but tastefully decorated. They had a long talk. Nicky liked Bob and Bob liked Nicky.

'My birthday's coming up,' said Bob at the end of their long discussion. 'It's on June 10th. Have you any brothers or sisters?'

'Yes, a brother and two sisters,' said Nicky now becoming bored with the long discussion about Bob's overdraft.

Bob shoved a long thick cigar into his mouth, undid the top two buttons of his shirt and loosened his tie. He took a sip of the champagne which he and Nicky had been drinking, took off his shoes and put his feet on an occasional table.

'Your brother and two sisters — what are their names and do they live in this country?'

'My older brother, Adrian, is covering a story in America for the *Telegraph*. My sister, Harriet, is in New York. My youngest sister is in London.'

Bob took another sip of champagne and lit his cigar which had gone out.

'Your sister in London — what's her name?'

'Eleanor. She's the one I'm closest to.'

'I'd like you to bring her to my birthday party on June 10th. Does she look like you?' he added suddenly.

'Come on Bob, that's a hard question. She's blonde but apart from that, I suppose you could say she looks like me.'

'She sounds lovely. For Christ's sake bring her along, Nicholas.'

* * *

1

Nicky drove me over to Headington Hill Hall. I had absolutely no idea what this was going to mean to me for the rest of my life. I had rather an ugly necklace but my sister-in-law, Marina — Adrian's wife, that is — wound it in circles round my wrist making it look like an attractive bracelet.

Nicky introduced me to Bob who was standing in a marquee, wearing a white bath towel dressing-gown. It was so dark that I couldn't see his face properly. He was very nice and friendly and it suddenly dawned on me that he generated a vivid, brutal, astonishing and overpowering sexuality.

'I like your bracelet,' he said, and touched it to see what it was made of.

'How many children have you got, Bob? My mother said you had a big family.'

'Seven,' said Bob. 'I'm afraid I used to have nine. My youngest daughter, Karine, died of leukaemia and my eldest son, Michael, died following a car accident. He was in a coma for a long time before we lost him.'

I thought I noticed his voice falter a little when he was giving me this information.

'Oh, I'm so sorry!'

He waved his left hand in the air a trifle dismissively as if to contain emotion. He continued: 'So Philip is my eldest son now. He's a student. Then there is my Annie — she is a blonde like you. After that come my twins Isabel and Christine.'

I noticed a note of pride in his voice when he referred to 'my twins'. It was a tone of almost childlike endearment which made me feel a surge of affection towards this big man with his guttural Cossack's laugh and deep musical voice.

At the time I had no idea that his twins had hovered between life and death in infancy and that Bob had driven like one possessed on to the pavements through the bumpy, cobbled streets of Paris, looking for the nearest hospital where they were saved, only by a hair's breadth from the Reaper's clutches.

'And your other children?'

'Oh yes, the others. There's my son Ian. Next in age comes Kevin and then there is my little one, Ghislaine. She was born about the time my Michael died. She is a little terror!'

The band suddenly lashed out with some heavy jazz — not that I care for jazz, but because I was with Bob I felt just as elevated as I would have been had I been listening to my favourite stuff, Russian folk music.

Bob led me by the hand to the centre of the floor. He became very animated and twirled me round and round. He didn't know that I had suffered from vertigo all my life, so much so that I have never even been able to ride a bicycle or climb a ladder.

'Stop it Bob! I'm going to fall over.'

'No you're not. All I have to do is turn you the other way.' He did and it worked. 'Feeling better?'

'Yes. Turning the other way was a good idea.'

'All my ideas are good ones,' he said. 'And I've got another one.'

'What's that?'

'Go into the swimming hut and get into a bathing suit.' He gave his guttural laugh again and I had a resounding slap on the behind. 'When you've found a bathing suit, come back and see me.'

The swimming hut Bob had referred to consisted of a sauna, a sunbed, a shower, basins and another room with a lot of bathing-suits strewn over the floor. I picked up the only one I could find which wasn't wet. It was a tight bathing-suit which I suspected must have belonged to 'little Ghislaine'. I struggled to drag it on to myself. I must have looked a mess and lacked the courage to look at myself in the mirror.

'Always dress to please men and not yourself,' someone had advised me once.

I went outside to find Bob. I looked dreadful. The garment would have made the bathing-suit Christine Keeler wore at Cliveden look like an outsized maternity dress.

I saw Bob in the distance. He had wandered off to another part of the garden. Multicoloured fireworks lit up the clear star spattered June sky, forming the words 'Happy Birthday Bob.' He seemed utterly devoid of self-consciousness or shyness. He was looking upwards at the flashing lights, smiling like a boy.

'Well Bob, does this bathing suit meet with your approval?'

He laughed. 'You look smashing!'

These words flooded into my ears like a massive shot of heroin. He picked me up without warning and carried me to the swimming-pool, laughing while I protested pathetically.

'What's wrong, can't you swim?'

'Oh yes,' I said, 'but I don't want to go in now.'

'Come on, don't be such a mean old spoilsport!' I couldn't say anything to that. He threw me into the heated water and watched me swimming round the circular pool, laughing and chewing an unlit cigar.

I went on swimming round the pool. I got tired and swam to the edge, clutching the ground above me with both hands.

'Hullo! I know all about you, you're Eléanore, aren't you? Bob has been telling me all about you. I'm Betty, Bob's wife. He told me how well he has been getting on with you. Any friend of Bob's is a friend of mine. Welcome to my home. Are you enjoying yourself?'

'Yes, thank-you. I'm having a very good time. I'm pleased to meet you.'

I extended my hand to shake hands with Betty. Again I couldn't see her face clearly in the dark but I noticed the beautiful dress she wore, together with her strong French accent. I warmed to her on sight.

I stretched out my hand for a little while waiting for her handshake. Instead she put two barbecued sausages into my hand.

'They are fresh from the barbecue, Eléanore. Be sure to eat them before they get cold.'

God, what a lion of a man and what a resplendent rose of a woman! and what an honour to have become the friend of both of them! Betty knew that many a woman fancied Bob, but it was above her to be jealous. She was proud. In her giving and glorious life she has known neither vindictiveness, envy nor malice. All she has ever cared about has been making other people happy.

I had had quite a lot to drink by the time Nicky took me home.

'I heard about how well you hit it off with the Bouncing Czech,' said Nicky.' He certainly got on with you. I'll arrange for you to meet again if you want.'

I was beginning to drift into sleep. I had a dream that this dazzling hulk of a man was leading me by the hand to his bedroom to the accompanyment of Handel's *Saraband Duo* in D minor, but I forced myself awake, aware of my loyalty to Betty, whom I had already come to see as a friend as well.

* * *

It was in the late sixties that there was some ominous talk about another airport being built in Buckinghamshire. Bob was the MP for North Bucks and pressure was being put on him to be more vehement in his public speeches to condemn the airport. Trees, scattered all over Buckinghamshire, were pasted with drawings of livid, violent looking farmers, viciously brandishing pitchforks. Captions underneath read 'Airport! not over our dead bodies.' I certainly wouldn't have liked to meet one of these farmers on a dark night.

Nicky and I told the family about how much I enjoyed myself at the Maxwells'. He also told my father about the friendship which had developed so spontaneously between Bob and me.

My father was concerned about the airport. Had it been built, pretty well all the residents of Buckinghamshire would have had to leave their homes.

I have always been close to my father, a shy, kindly, quiet, serious, hard working, intellectually-brilliant, good-humoured, but stubborn man. Once he gets an idea into his head he sticks to it like a terrier with a rubber ball in its mouth and will not falter. This, I attribute to the fact that he is Welsh.

He and I were sitting in the dining-room after lunch.

'I know all about you and Bob,' he said.

'You talk as if there has been impropriety. I can assure you there hasn't.'

'I don't mean that. I know about your friendship but the reason I mention this is certainly not my motive for saying what I have to say. I have nothing against your friendship.'

'Well, is there some kind of problem?'

My father inhaled deeply on his cigarette and, as he sucked in the nicotine, he made a slight wheezing noise which troubled me.

'Well, what's all this about?' I asked.

'It's all this business about the airport, which would mean that the whole of Buckinghamshire would be uninhabitable.'

I poured myself some more wine.

'I understand that but I don't really see what I can do about it.'

'I'll tell you,' my father said. 'To fight this airport we need funds. So far, we haven't heard a word from Uncle Bob.'

I drank some more wine.

'Well, if you like, I don't mind going over to see him,' I said. 'I'll ask him for funds. I know he will pay if I ask him.'

My father looked out of the corner of his eye, half suspiciously, half amused.

'Oh, so you're as close as that, are you?'

'Don't be silly. As I told you there has never been any impropriety and there never will. I'll ring him up this afternoon and I'll invite myself over to tea. Then I'll ask him for the money. How much do you want me to ask him for?'

'Five thousand pounds.'

'Oh,' I said, 'well I'll do my best.'

My father and I left the room. I picked up the phone and dialled Bob's number.

'Bob, is that you?'

'Yes.'

'I will be coming over for tea with you later this afternoon, if I may.'

'Yes, of course you can, Missy. I'll tell everyone to expect you. You will be most welcome.'

Our family chauffeur was called Mr Brightwell. I am afraid he is dead now. Before I tell you about Mr Brightwell's memorable encounter with Bob, I will have to say a few things about Mr Brightwell first.

He looked like a little gnome and had such a murderous temper when provoked that he would have made Ivan the Terrible seem like the chairman of a home for birds with broken wings, and a rabid bull like a sedated lamb.

I am sorry to confess that though sickly, I was an exceptionally naughty child — that is before I was sent to boarding school, and I am bound to say my behaviour improved only fractionally after that.

I can't tell you what supreme pleasure it gave me to make Mr Brightwell angry. When he was in a bait he would scream and stamp on the garage floor like Rumplestiltskin and occasionally throw a spanner at the luckless person who had upset him. He looked so funny that I was hooked on driving him into a rage.

One morning, I noticed he had got ready a bowl of clean oil to pour into my father's car. I got hold of a bucket of gravel and poured it into the bowl of oil. His rage was indescribable.

'If you don't get out of me garridge, I'll take you by the 'and to your mother!'

'No such luck. She's in London.'

Underneath his violent temper, I have to hand it to him, he had a heart of gold. I got into the car to go to the Maxwells.

'Where's Headington Hill Hall?' he asked.

'Turn right at the bottom of the drive and I'll direct you from there.'

Mr Brightwell, though extremely friendly when not provoked was silent throughout the journey and so was I.

He took me down the sinuous heavily ramped drive towards Headington Hill Hall.

'I understand you was only invited to tea,' said Mr Brightwell. 'I hope you're not going to dawdle. I missed *Dad's Army* last week and I'll be blowed if I am going to miss it again.'

I saw a group of men talking at the bottom of the drive just outside the house. There were at least ten of them. Because I hadn't looked at Bob's face the last time we met in the dark, I was temporarily unsure who he was. I approached one of the men.

'Take me to Mr Maxwell, please. Mr Robert Maxwell.'

The man did as I asked. It is not at all in my nature to be shy since I tend towards exhibitionism. But on this occasion I did feel rather shy and when this mood takes me over, I tend to shout at the top of my voice and stare at the ground.

Bob wore a beige overcoat. The hot air from his mouth formed clouds in the cold March air. For some inexplicable reason, I found this attractive.

'My father sent me here to ask you for £5,000,' I said, my voice raised and my eyes still on the ground.

So far, I had not seen his face properly.

'Who is your father and what does he want the money for?'

'For the anti-Airport campaign.'

I raised my head and saw his face. A feeble March sun shone through the trees, making his jet-black eyes look hazel. His was about the most beautiful face I have ever seen, radiant, god-like and essentially masculine. When his facial muscles creased into a smile, he shone more gloriously than the sun itself.

Vertigo which has plagued me all my life, descended on me yet again. The trees, Bob and the men with him started to circle slowly round and gather speed like a roundabout. The last thing I saw before I lost consciousness was the beautiful smiling face of the man from whom I had been asked to extract money.

I had no idea where I was when I woke up. The room was dark and the blinds were drawn. I felt very sick for a while but the feeling passed. I recognized Betty who came into the room with a tray of tea and some cakes.

'Whatever has happened?' I asked.

'There is no need to worry. You were outside in the drive talking to Bob. It was clear you hadn't had anything to eat beforehand. He said you were cold and white before you fell.'

I then realized where I was and why I was there. I remembered that Mr Brightwell had implored me not to be too long because he wanted to watch *Dad's Army*.

Betty sat and talked to me, first in English, then in French. She said how welcome I was to stay in her house at any time. Then she turned off the light and told me to rest. She said Bob would be in to see me later.

'Well then, Missy,' he began. (Sometimes he called me 'Missy', sometimes 'Pussycat' and occasionally 'Basso Profundo' due to my deep voice.)

'I am not ill, I just fell over, that's all.'

He looked puzzled and suggested calling a doctor. My thoughts went immediately to Mr Brightwell's wrath due to missing *Dad's Army*. Because I was older, I was no longer amused by his tantrums. I feared them.

'There is a chauffeur outside waiting for me,' I said. 'He'll be furious if he misses *Dad's Army*.'

Bob brushed a stray lock of black hair from his forehead.

'F*** *Dad's Army*!' he said, his voice raised. 'I've had the rare pleasure to meet you twice and apart from your good looks I don't know a damned thing about you. I know about your family and that your father owns the *Telegraph* but I don't know anything about you as a person. What are your interests?'

'Russian music, Russian literature, piano playing and the Communist Party.'

At that time I was a dotty, starry-eyed Communist and I told him, not without considerable pride that I was a member of the Communist Party.

'Have you been to Russia?'

'Yes, I went there last winter.'

'Who with?' he demanded suddenly.

'I went alone.'

'Alone?' He looked as if he had swallowed a bee. I couldn't understand his astonishment.

'Yes, why not? I do a lot of things alone.'

He stared me in the face. Had I not been lying down I might have fainted again.

'Christ, I have never seen such guts and yet you are scared of your chauffeur's rage if he misses bloody *Dad's Army*!'

'I am not scared. He missed it last week as well. The only thing I am scared of in life is illness.'

He ignored this.

'Wait a minute, Missy,' he said, 'I have something to show you.'

Five minutes later he came in with a pile of beautifully bound Russian books by Pushkin, Gorky and Gogol. How I wished I spoke more Russian then. I made up my mind that I would teach myself the language.

'Accept this as my esteem for your beauty, your guts and your company.'

I thought I was about to faint again but I controlled myself by biting my tongue.

'They are all beautiful. You *are* 'kind'!'

'I am not kind!' he said with peculiar certainty. 'Would you like me to read to you a little?'

'But what about that chauffeur outside ...'

'F*** the chauffeur outside! What would you like me to read?'

'Tatyana's conversation with her nanny from *Yevgeni Oengin*.'

'I admire the resolution with which you make up your mind.'

He opened the book in exactly the right place without delay and read the sad verses about a woman crossed in love. His Russian accent was neither Moscow nor Leningrad. It was strange with rather a rustic lilt.

I knew the words of the scene by heart, and the heroine's helplessness, together with Bob's phenomenal beauty, caused the odd tear to stray down my cheeks. He swiftly wiped it away with the back of his hand.

'Will you sign these books, Bob?' I gave him a pen and he did as he was asked.

'To Eleanor with admiration.' I suddenly noticed he was left-handed and, without having the slightest idea why, I felt another surge of excitement, maybe because I knew him to be different from others.

'Now for the cheque for your dad.' He wrote it out and put it into an envelope. I didn't see the amount.

'Right, Missy, it is time you got up. Then we can have tea. Perhaps your driver would like to join us. What's his name?'

'Mr Brightwell.'

'Mr Lightweight — did you say?'

I had uncontrollable giggles.

'What's so funny?'

'No, it's Brightwell, not Lightweight.'

It was already dark. Mr Brightwell was sitting in my father's navy-blue, somewhat hearse-like Ford estate, smoking cigarettes and looking at a tabloid paper showing photographs of naked women.

Bob banged peremptorily on the window. I must point out that he related far more easily to women than members of his own sex so his handling of the highly peppery Mr Brightwell was the opposite of the way he treated me.

'You there, sitting in your vehicle, looking at pictures of naked women,' boomed Bob, as if Mr Brightwell were sitting 50 yards away, 'what are you reading?'

An expression of rage clouded over Mr Brightwell's gnome-like face. I got the giggles.

'Mind your own flippin' business, Sir!'

Bob ignored the remark.

'I'd like you to come into my house and have tea with me and my wife,' said Bob but his words sounded more like a command than a social invitation.

Mr Brightwell's appalling temper worsened and he went purple in the face, fanatically taking off his cap and putting it on again. He turned his head towards Bob, his eyes almost coming out of their sockets. I struggled desperately to keep a straight face.

'I'll have you know that I have served the Berry family, man and boy and the Smith family before that!' he bellowed in a homicidal rage.' It was my privilege to groom Lord Birkenhead's horses!'

Bob appeared puzzled by his aggression and must have wondered why an invitation to tea had made another man so livid.

'B***ger what you did to Lord Birkenhead's horses!' said Bob, this time very impatiently. 'Get out of your vehicle and come into my house to have tea with Eleanore, my wife and me.'

Mr Brightwell put his cap on and threw his paper on to the floor of the car. He put out his cigarette and got out very hesitantly, staring lividly at Bob as he moved. He walked slowly into the house with his head lowered as if he were walking behind a bier.

Bob led us into a room with Empire furniture, a harp and a piano. Mr Brightwell was introduced to Betty to whom he was stiffly courteous. She offered him some cakes which she had made herself and which he refused, and tea which he accepted, sitting on the edge of his chair throughout.

Bob asked Mr Brightwell a number of inoffensive questions delivered with the arresting and startling intonation characteristic of him and was answered with monosyllables. To this day I have never been able to work out whether his answers were due to rage that he had missed *Dad's Army* or grossly atypical reticence.

We got up to go, I hugged both the Maxwells and had a kiss on the mouth from Bob.*

Mr Brightwell walked out first. Bob took me aside.

'God, that chauffeur of yours is a scary fellow! I wouldn't like to meet him alone on a dark night.'

That set me off again; my giggles were uncontrollable.

*Not a lingering kiss

'It doesn't take much to get you going,' said Bob.

'You don't understand how comical he is when he gets in a rage,' I said. 'When I was small I used to pour gravel into his bowl of clean oil, just to see his furious face and get him to throw a spanner at my head.'

'Missy, you're bloody barmy!'

On the way home I tried to break the stony silence.

'What did you think of Mr Maxwell, Mr Brightwell?'

'No comment!' he barked.

It was fairly late by the time I got home. My mother was upstairs. My father was waiting for me, sitting by the fire.

'Have you got the money? What took you so long?'

I passed the sealed envelope to my father. When he opened it he appeared irritated.

'This amount falls short of the £5,000 I asked you to get from Bob,' he said.

'I can't help that. I went over there, didn't I? It was very nice of him to give you money at all.'

My father looked puzzled.

'You still didn't tell me why you were away for so long. Did any impropriety take place between you?'

'No.'

I fondled the lovely signed books under my arm with pride. They and not the money were the trophies of my expedition.

'I was away for so long because I made the mistake of looking Bob in the eye. It's true I had met him before in the dark but I didn't see his face. In daylight he was so extraordinarily good-looking that I fainted and I had to be put to bed.'

'You fainted?'

'Yes. I inherit occasional fainting attacks from you.'

'Well a fat lot of good you are, dear, if on promising to ask a man for money, you faint when you look at him!'

He saw that I was becoming irritated and he must have felt that his words were unfairly uttered.

'All the same it was very sporting of you to do what you did, even though you didn't get as much money as I would have liked.'

I rang Bob up and thanked him for his kindness.

'You know you have a permanent invitation to my house,' he said.' You can stay as long as you want when you want. Betty and I look upon you as being one of our children.'

I suffered from schizophrenia in my teens. The disease is the vilest affliction that can affect anyone because it is worse than physical pain. Your hallucinations, both auditory and visual, are terrifying. Voices tell you to do things that you know are unwise and when you do these things you have no idea you have done them afterwards, and yet you are obliged to accept blame for them.

Part of the disease was a conflict about having joined the Communist Party and I began to lose faith in its ideals when I read about Russian intellectuals being sent to labour camps, simply because they were not Communists.

I didn't want to believe what I read. One morning, my mother arranged to meet me in *Aldo Bruno's*, just about the most prestigious hairdresser's in Mayfair. I came in, making quite some noise in my high heels (I was about 16 at the time). I had a bundle of rolled-up newspapers under my arm. The top newspaper on my pile was *The Morning Star* (a Communist newspaper).

I greeted my mother, sat down beside her and started reading it. Hairdressers stared at us, giggling. They knew instinctively that I was both annoying and embarrassing my mother.

Had she not made so much noise, expressing her shock that I was reading a Communist newspaper in a Mayfair hairdresser's, (which is frequented by film stars, the aristocracy and newspaper proprietors' wives among others), she probably wouldn't have attracted so much attention to what I was reading.

Her voice was even louder and deeper than mine which is saying quite a lot. She picked the paper up and waved it in the air.

'Where in the world did you find this?'

'I bought it,' I said, my voice almost as loud as hers.

'Why did you buy it?'

'Because I like it.'

'Why do you like it?'

'Why?' I said loudly. 'I like its content, I like its editorials and I like its reasoning.'

Aldo Bruno himself, who owned the hairdresser's and who lacked any sense of humour, allowed his mouth to gape open like an owl waiting to be fed, and dropped his scissors on the floor.

'I can see she won't be coming in here again,' he said, I thought very unpleasantly.

'You do see I have an awful lot to put up with,' said my mother, her voice uncharacteristically low like a catholic making confession.

It was when my mother and I were walking across the street to her car that she really began to take off. First, she spoke (loudly enough to be heard in Bayswater) about farmers under Stalin being collectivized and the horror of the labour camps from which barely anyone emerged alive.

Flabbergasted passers-by formed a circle around us to listen to her overtly articulate condemnation of the perils of Russian communism. Suddenly, she added as if as an afterthought:

'Do you realize Lady Glendevon, the Marchioness of Salisbury and Lady Rothermere were all in there today? You've made a laughing stock of us both!'

I must, however, hand it to her that she turned the whole episode into a joke when the family were gathered, using maximum hyperbole.

* * *

'Do you mind if we have Bob to lunch on Sunday?' This was my brother, Nicky asking. 'Besides, I want to find out why the hell he wants to buy The *News of the World*.'

'Yes, by all means ask him,' said my mother. 'After all, he has been very kind to Eleanor, giving her all those books like that.'

Bob came over, minus Betty but with his identical twin daughters, Isabel and Christine. He wore a fur hat and trench-like overcoat and looked distinctly Russian. He sat next to my mother at lunch and I sat on his other side. I looked at him out of the corner of my eye and could hardly eat.

Suddenly, he turned to me. I was feeling a little shy which he sensed. He wanted to bring me into the conversation.

'Are you keen on opera?'

'Yes, some operas at any rate. *Carmen*'s my favourite and I like *La Traviata* and *The Magic Flute*.'

'I admire the extent of your knowledge. Are you interested in politics?'

My mother spoke before I did.

'She's a Communist, you know. She needs to read *The Morning Star* every day just as a Chinaman needs rice!'

' So you're a Communist, are you?' He sounded strangely impressed.

'And she's a card carrying member of the Communist Party. She carries great bouquets of flowers to the Russian Embassy on Lenin's birthday every year.'

Bob looked approvingly at me but I couldn't understand why.

13

Perhaps he thought I was eccentric and had a penchant for eccentric women.

'My God, what amazing guts!' he exclaimed.

* * *

It was not long afterwards that schizophrenia struck me down. Apart from confusion about Communism, it was precipitated by about twenty different causes none of which I intend to strain myself, or my readers, by listing. I am, however, cured. My compulsory hospitalization was brought about by the following singularly trivial incident:

A dear friend called Peter Van Praagh* gave me a gold cigarette case for my birthday. The only thing he left out was an engraving. I had rather a good idea. There's an old Russian song that I like which has the advantage of a chorus being interchangeable with English words: Nye zhivoi v styeppi, chellovyek lezhit

Okol myotvovo voron kruzhit (but in Cyrillic letters of course). The direct English words for the chorus are: *In the steppe a dead man lies. Round the man a raven flies.*

All my life, my tastes have veered towards the macabre and I went straight to a jeweller, being ignorant of his amateurishness, while waiting for a train at Paddington Station on my way to stay with the Maxwells.

The thin, scruffy, bearded man standing behind the counter was unattractive and unfriendly but I decided not to go anywhere else because I wanted to show the gift to the Maxwells who often invited me to stay with them on my birthday.

'Yes?' said the man.

This immediately made me hostile and aggressive.

'See this gold cigarette case I've got here?'

The man scratched his unkempt beard.

'What about it?' he asked in a taciturn tone.

'I'm about to tell you. Here is a piece of paper with writing on it in English. I've written the words in capitals but I want them transcribed in italics.

'There's another thing I'll have to point out to you and that is that the word 'steppe' is not spelt S-T-E-P but S-T-E-P-P-E.'

I had such an instinctive dislike for this man that I couldn't control the arrogance in my voice.

---

* Peter Van Praagh: model for Joseph Slandisch from *Your Father Died on the Gallows*. He took his life in March 1988 but had the courtesy to purchase fifteen copies of my *Never Alone with Rex Malone* first.

14

'That's bloomin' stupid,' he said. " 'Course it's S-T-E-P!"

By this time my dislike for the man had turned to hatred. I did not feel like lecturing him patiently on Russian literature or geography.

'I don't intend to explain or give reasons why I want it
spelt that way. I am merely adamant that it be S-T-E-P-P-E and not the most obvious spelling. I've made my instructions perfectly clear. I do not need to justify them since I'm the one who's paying you. I'll be gone for half an hour and I will expect the work to be done to my satisfaction when I come back. If you do not carry out my instructions, you will not be paid.'

I was about to slap the cigarette case on the counter but he beat me to it by snatching it from my hand.

'See you get it right!'

I walked out. I felt happy that day because I was on my way to see the Maxwells, and when it was my birthday, I was always allowed to sit on Bob's right and be the centre of his attention. Some people feared doing this because of his sudden way of asking penetrating questions. It never bothered me, though, because I had learnt that he liked his guests, particularly women, to bark at him in reply. Sometimes, when women barked at him or snapped his head off, he would collapse in hysterical giggles like a child. If a woman barked at him too loudly, however, he would go into what seemed to be an angry silence. I caused him to do the latter three times later in his life and when I did I felt guilty and unhappy afterwards.

These were some of the thoughts passing through my mind as I sat in a coffee bar at Paddington waiting for the jeweller to complete his task. For some reason or other the strong coffee I'd had, deepened my hostility towards him and I became increasingly suspicious that he had damaged my property. I entered his shop, treading heavily, staring the man in the eye as I went towards him.

'OK, let's see your work.'

He slapped it on the counter.

'Fifteen pounds,' he said and stretched out his hand, palm upwards, like a down-market Dikensian debt-collector.

'When I see my property, you'll get your money.'

I picked it up and examined it, holding it under the Anglepoise lamp precariously balanced at the edge of the counter.

Even I did not believe he had done the one thing I had told him not to do. He had engraved 'step' deliberately and had also carved the quotation in capitals when I had asked for italics.

I simply don't know exactly what I did next. My eyes must have rolled back because all I could see was red. I realized that, even in my unathletic state, I had pushed the lamp on the floor and vaulted over the counter. My rage was so intense that the violence within me brought bile to my mouth. I screamed and shouted abuse and to this day I have no idea what I said.

Suddenly, I realized there was blood on the man. It frightened me that I had no recollection of how it had got there. The man was screaming and I saw a small stream of blood running down his neck. I had bitten his ear. The shock surged over me quite slowly. The next thing I saw was that the shop was full of cops.

I have usually had the gift of the gab and realized I had to get my word in first if I was to get to the Maxwells for lunch.

I strode towards the cop who had the greater number of stripes on his arm. I chose the most verbose language possible to bore my listeners although my voice was trembling like a leaf.

'Good morning, sir,' I said, 'I'm ever so sorry to have called you and your worthy colleagues out on this nice warm May morning but first, I must emphasize one very important point: 'I'm not fully cognizant of how familiar you are with Russian literature and geographical factors pertaining thereto, but I must point out to you that in Russia, particularly in Eastern Russia, there are vast endless plains interspersed occasionally by very tall gaunt mottled-trunked birch trees which are referred to as the "Steppes".'

The cop gaped at me as if he had swallowed a bee. He opened his mouth to speak but no words came. I was afraid he might get round to interrupting me so I continued.

'The extent of your knowledge about the Steppes is, I regret, unknown to me but if you do not know about either them or the poetry relating to them, I would be most indebted to you for allowing me to familiarize you with another extremely important point.

'The word "steppe", when describing the Russian Steppes which I have already touched on in passing, is not spelt S-T-E-P as a person unfamiliar with Russian literature and geography might think. It is very specifically spelt S-T-E-P-P-E. Now that I have furnished you with this reasonably unimportant but necessary information to enable you to proceed with your daily commitments, I will now endeavour to inform you of the precise circumstances leading to your encounter with me.'

'I don't want to hear all this pompous, potty talk!' snapped the cop. 'Why's that man got blood on him? What did you do to him?'

'I believe he fell. Also he swindled me and did serious damage to my property for which I intend to sue him. I'm bored with this incident. I've got to catch my train.'

'Oh, and where do you think you're going?'

'To the Maxwells, of course. Where else?'

'You're not, you know. You've committed a serious offence.'

The odious man told his side of the story, deliberately lying throughout. As is sometimes the case in the lives of people doing what I did, I was 'sectioned.' Two bent shrinks signed a bogus form to indicate I was batty and after that I was binned. A thick needle was pushed into my arm where white-coated sadists held me steady. The needle contained a substance called Largactil which induces suicidal depression and turns you into a vegetable.

Once I was limp, strait-jacketed and obviously unable to struggle, they tried to take details from me. I said I was 21 as opposed to 17 and that my parents, whom I didn't want informed, were touring round America and there was no way to get hold of them. I gave my brother Nicky's name as my next of kin, he being the calmest of my three siblings. Adrian would have been very confused and embarrassed that I had injured the jeweller and Harriet would have given me a long lecture about it which was one thing I didn't want, seeing I had been pumped up to the eyeballs with that vile and terrifying drug.

My mind came to a halt. I had no feelings at all. I could neither laugh nor cry and I was no longer aware that it was my birthday. I had no idea how long they had kept me in that horrific whitewashed room on my own or how long I had been subjected to the fear and loneliness my wicked captors imposed on me.

Among the dreadful things this dreadful drug did to me was to give me terrifying hallucinations. When I opened a drawer, I saw a decapitated baby in it. Once, when I was taken to the bathroom, I saw a hanged man covered in blood.

When Nicky came to see me, my first reaction was one of relief but the profound depression induced in me by regular injections of Largactil made me unaware of reality and destroyed my will to ask him to get me out.

The depression deepened alarmingly. The shrinks continued to fill me with Largactil and decided I should have electric shock therapy for the depression. It did not occur to either of them to work out what was causing it. The electric shocks made it worse than ever. I began to work out a plan to take my life. Somehow, the nurses were aware of this. For

17

several days they took it in turns to sit with me day and night to make sure I didn't bump myself off.

I had no idea of what was going on outside. At about 1.30 p.m. on 6 May, Nicky received a somewhat peremptory call. It was the rich, rounded, slightly northern-sounding voice of Robert Maxwell, booming dark red velvet down the line.

'Where the hell's that sister of yours, Nicholas? We're giving a lunch for her and she hasn't turned up. Damn it, I've been looking forward to seeing her and I've got to go to Moscow later this afternoon for a week.'

Nicky tried to explain the situation as delicately as possible.

'Sorry, Bob but something very odd happened this morning at Paddington Station. Apparently my sister got into a fight with a man about the spelling of a word on an engraved cigarette case. My sister attacked this man and injured him.'

'What the hell are you talking about, Nicholas?'

'My sister has had to go to hospital.'

'You mean the man harmed her?'

'I can't discuss it now. When do you get back from Moscow?'

'In a week, for Christ's sake. Is she seriously hurt?'

'No. But I'll have to talk to you urgently when you come back.'

'Why do you say "urgently" having said she's not seriously hurt?'

'I'm afraid my sister is mentally ill.'

'Mentally bloody ill? No she isn't.'

'She's in an asylum. Perhaps you're the only person who can help her. The psychiatrists are making her worse.'

'Listen, Nicholas, I'll call you as soon as I'm back. Be sure to leave a number where I can get you. Give me the numbers of the f***ing psychiatrists involved. Do her parents know?'

'No.'

'That's not important. I'll sort it out myself. Look after her when I'm away.'

To this day, I have no idea of the whereabouts of the asylum. It may have been in North London somewhere because 20 years later when travelling through North London, I had a sudden unexplained attack of death-like misery and palpitations.

It is also known that unless a depression is not drug- induced, electric shock treatment can't disperse it. In fact, if the electric shocks are applied every day intensively for more than a week, the brain can be irreparably damaged and the patient just as good as dead.

The switchboard at the hospital was jammed with calls from Moscow. Bob demanded to speak to both the shrinks. Although he had had no medical training, he might possibly have been psychic — a gift inherited from his mother, Hannah Hoch who raised him in the village of Solotvino in the Carpathian Mountains where he was born. She herslf was psychic and when Bob was only 2 she predicted that he would live to be internationally known.

Bob somehow knew that a combination of high dose anti-psychotic drugs and electric shock treatment would be lethal if prolonged. By about the fifth day, I had sunk further still until I reached catatonia. Nicky was terrified and called Bob on his car phone while he was coming home from Heathrow Airport.

'My sister's worse, Bob! I don't know what to do. The GP's I've consulted say they don't know as much as psychiatrists do.'

'For Christ's sake, calm down, Nicholas! No problem is solved by panicking. Remind me of the name and whereabouts of this f***ing asylum.'

Nicky told him.

'Nicholas!'

'Yes.'

'Stay where you are and don't do anything. I'll get my driver to take me there straight away.'

Bob's driver's name was Mr Hoppitt. He was none too bright but at least he had a pretty insensitive hide and a sense of humour which is why Bob kept him. Bob got out a map and directed Hoppitt to the asylum. He always liked him to drive fast and Hoppitt must have screeched to a halt outside, judging by the skid marks on the gravel.

Bob strode into the asylum wearing a white flannel suit and what looked like a northern coal-miner's check cloth cap. Even in my drugged state, I heard his velvet voice booming all the way down the corridor, but in my confusion, I didn't think it was real. When he asked where I was, he was told straight away. There were some male nurses outside in the corridor but it's likely he scared them to death which is why they did nothing to stop him.

My door was a good 4 inches thick. It was locked. Bob heaved his weight against it some twenty times like a battering ram. In the end, it gave way like even the strongest things do to a physically and psycho-logically powerful man. He was like Rambo. No challenge was ever too much for him.

I was sitting on the floor of the padded whitewashed room. The treatment was so heinous that all I could do was yearn for death to come quickly. I didn't recognize Bob at first because I was so doped so I stared at him vacantly, hardly able to take it in that it was him.

'It's all right, Missy. I'm taking you away.'

'Best to leave me to die.'

Bob got impatient. I can't remember what he said though. He jerked me to my feet and tore the strait-jacket off with his strong hands as if it were made of paper. For some reason, the first thing I noticed were his hands. They were very small for a man of his size and delicate-looking like a woman's hands. I couldn't understand why such small, gentle-looking hands could wield the strength of Samson. I was also struck by the sweetness of his breath and his extreme physical cleanliness.

'Dress, Missy. We haven't got all day. I'll look the other way.'

At first I had no idea where my clothes were. Bob must have known because he pointed to a cupboard. The clothes were lying on the floor because there were no coat-hangers. I wandered about naked, falling over like a drunk while he stood in the corner with his back to me. I pulled on some white fishnet tights, patent black sling-back high-heeled shoes, a navy blue sleeveless minidress and a thin, white polo-necked shirt to go underneath it. There was no mirror so I couldn't put on any make-up. I found a gold watch in the corner of the cupboard and a gold pendant to go round my neck.

I steadied myself by holding the iron bedstead.

'You can turn round now, Bob.'

He did and smiled.

'You look smashing, but your hair doesn't.'

He took a comb from his inside pocket and tidied my long tangled hair like a nanny. That's the one thing he wasn't so good at. He couldn't negotiate the knots and tangles.

'Leave it, Bob. It's OK. Besides, you're pulling.'

'OK, OK. Come on, Eleanore.' (He always pronounced by name with its stress on the last syllable.) 'I've other things to do besides dawdle in a bloody place like this doing women's hair,' he said half smiling. 'We've got to get the hell out of here!'

I could hardly walk because of the toxicity of the drugs combined with the other treatment. As soon as I had nothing to hold on to, I fell over.

'Help me, Bob. It's the bloody drugs.'

'You should never have got yourself in here. You bit a man at Paddington Station, I heard. Douglas someone or other, they said his name was. When the police came, you gave them a 2 hour lecture about the bloody Russian steppes. What the hell had you taken?'

'I can't remember the incident at all.'

'It was your birthday — you were on your way to Betty and me.'

'Oh yes, I remember going to the station. Nothing else.'

He wasn't all that interested in the incident, I didn't think. He put out his arm.

'Hold on to me and come with me.'

If it hadn't been for the fact that the crucifying depression was still on me, crushing my brain like a metal clamp and making me feel as if I were at the bottom of a well unable to get out, I would have found the whole episode comical.

Burly male nurses and sadistic beady-eyed female nurses, who had been so cruel and treated me like a dog, stared transfixed at us as if they had seen a vision. They were all terrified of Bob and couldn't move. Regardless of my black state of mind, I looked at him in wonder, fascinated by his power to petrify others just by looking at them. I would have given anything to have that gift.

I held his arm with both hands to steady myself and kept my eyes lowered, fearing these nurses who never spoke to me except to humiliate me and who pushed sausages and mashed potatoes inside my cell through a hatch as a zoo-keeper feeds a caged lion.

'*Yea though I walk through the valley of the shadow of death, I will fear no evil: for thou art with me; thy rod and thy staff they comfort me,*' I said out loud.

'Shut up, Ellie! I've been travelling all night. I don't want a load of the Scriptures thrown at me now!'

He guided me down the steps outside the great grim and desolate building. I stumbled but he tightened his grip on me with both hands, preventing me from falling.

The cheerful Mr Hoppitt sprung nimbly from the Rolls and opened the back door while Bob continued to hold me steady. He gave me a slap on the behind and pushed me in.

'We'll go to my house in Fitzroy Square,' said Bob, 'and can you get a move on.'

'I'll do my best, Mr Maxwell. I can't do more than that.'

Hoppitt was a stickler for observing the speed limit. I could feel Bob's frustration beside me.

Suddenly, he hit Hoppitt on the back of the head with a rolled up copy of the *Financial Times*. This was something he always did to drivers he thought were driving too slowly. Hoppitt was in a 30 m.p.h. zone. He increased his speed to 55 m.p.h. and was hauled into the side by a cop.

'Would you please get out of your car, sir. I'll see your licence while you're at it.'

Hoppitt got out and did as he was told. Bob also got out and eased himself into the driver's seat.

'Sorry, officer,' he said, 'I'm in a bastard of a hurry. You'll have to sort this out with my driver.'

He drove off leaving Hoppitt in with the cop. I thought it was a bit naughty of Bob but I was amused and got the giggles.

'What are you laughing at? I can see you in the mirror.'

'I like your style, Bob.'

We drove on in silence until we came to a traffic jam. Bob moved over to the right-hand side of the road and crashed along with his hand on the horn.

The telephone rang. I could hear a crisp female voice telling him there was a call from Rome. Bob spoke at length in French to the caller. His conversation was entirely about high finance, a subject which has always bored me. It was evident from his conversation that things weren't going the way he wished. Eventually, he hung up.

'So how's Rome, Bob?' I asked.

He looked strained and irritated.

'Rome stands where Rome stood, on the Tiber!'

The rest of the journey was in silence.

His house in Fitzroy Square was both dark and gloomy with sombre oak coloured panelling and poor lighting.

'You could do with a glass of champagne, Missy.'

He gave a spectacular wolf-whistle and a Filipino maid briskly entered the room.

'I'd prefer a Coca-Cola, Bob.'

'Come on! I can't be doing with people who don't drink alcohol. Why don't you become a nun?'

'You're right. I think I would rather have champagne.'

When the glass was passed to me, I drank it in one gulp in an effort to disperse the depression caused by the treatment.

'That's more like it, Missy!'

'I might as well have another.'

He filled my glass to the brim. I drained it in one go. I could feel the depression shifting even though this wouldn't be for long.

'I'll have another, if I may. I'm beginning to feel better.'

'All right but I'm only going to give you half. I'm taking you out to lunch and I don't want you passing out.'

He drove me to a busy prestigious restaurant somewhere in the City. We sat on the same side of the table, and to my relief, he ordered more champagne.

'Let's see how strong a head you've got. But don't knock it back all in one go, otherwise you'll be sick. He poured the champagne into my glass and told the waiter to bring two steaks and various other things.

'Let's have the truth, then,' he said suddenly before the lunch arrived. 'How did you really come to be so stupid as to have yourself put into that bloody hospital? I want your own version of events.'

'It was a trivial thing, really. A jeweller at Paddington Station stole a gold cigarette case I'd been given. I wanted something engraved on it and he refused to give it back to me. We had a fight and things went on from there.'

'You shouldn't be smoking anyway. It's bloody dangerous. I've had a lung removed because of it. To get back to what happened, what things went on from where, for Christ's sake?'

'My memory's not so good because of the drugs still in my system, I was put into the hands of a couple of bent shrinks.'

'Shrinks? What the hell are they?'

'Sorry, I meant psychiatrists.'

'You were a fool to get involved with them. Here you are, looking ill and in a bloody awful state, wasting your life.'

His booming voice reverberated throughout the crowded restaurant. Diners turned round to stare at us and I was proud to be seen with Bob. He went on still just as loudly.

'You've got looks. You've got brains. You've joined the Communist Party and even had the guts to go to Russia alone. Why don't you come and work for me?'

I was feeling better but certainly not at all well. The idea of committing myself to working for this man, whom I suspected was an exacting task master, gave me claustrophobia at this stage.

'I don't want to make a spontaneous decision,' I said. 'You'll have to give me time to think it over. Besides, I'm not quite fit enough to work yet. My psychiatrists say I've got schizophrenia.'

'What's wrong with that? B***** what your psychiatrists say, if you'll excuse my soldier's language.' Then in a much quieter tone he added gently. 'I've got schizophrenia too, Ellie. I've had it since the War. It certainly isn't a serious disease.'

'That's not right. It's terribly serious. Might I ask why you haven't been to a doctor about it?'

'I don't believe in bloody doctors!' he replied, his voice raised in anger. 'I've learnt to live with it.'

'May I ask what caused you to get it?'

'It was my past,' he said abruptly.

I looked sideways at him and saw that he looked profoundly haunted and disturbed as if he had been hit on a raw nerve.

'I'm sorry to hear that,' I said.

At that time, I had no idea that his family, who were Jewish Czechoslovaks, had been taken to Auschwitz and gassed alive. Among them, was his mother on whom he doted with a love almost on a par with that of Paul Morel for his mother in *Sons and Lovers*. Among them, too, was his grandfather who had taught him his bargaining ability and shrewd business sense. This man was the father figure in his life. He didn't get on with his own father who apparently was a bit of a bully (and this is a bit of an understatement).

Bob sat in a brooding silence lasting about 10 minutes. I drank more champagne because I felt the melancholia, inflicted on me by the hospital staff, returning.

'Waiter! Two Turkish coffees!'

The other diners, who obviously didn't have anything better to do than gape at a couple of gloomy eccentrics, all stopped talking.

The waiter brought the coffee to the table in a container but forgot to bring any sugar. The extra champagne was beginning to make me uninhibited.

'I want sugar, Bob.'

'You're right to say 'I want' instead of 'please may I have'. It puts others in awe of you and you can get what you want more quickly. A person too timid to say 'I want' gets nowhere. No doubt you've been taught otherwise but I'm rougher because I've had it rough. Waiter! Sugar!'

Sugar was brought to the table. It's quite a helpful agent in treating melancholia so I put four spoonfuls into the small cup provided.

'Christ, you've got a sweet tooth!' said Bob.

I sensed that his brooding mood had passed. I took his hand in mine which he appeared to like.

'Thanks for lunch, Bob. Where do you want to take me now?'

'To my house in Oxford. My wife, Betty and I are going to look after you until you are more under control. Nicholas is coming to dinner tonight. I'm sure you'll like that.'

'You've been so kind to me,' I said.

'I'm not kind! You've got something about you that I like and admire.'

'Oh! What's that?' I asked puzzled.

'I'll tell you what. You've got looks, you've got guts, you've got a nice sharp little tongue and you don't take any s*** from anyone!'

I felt a sudden glorious elixir pass through me. I knew that I worshipped Bob with every inch of my being.

'I can tell by my association with you that there will be nothing in life you want that you won't get. Just demand it and it will be yours.'

'You've got a loud deep voice designed to scare the wits out of everyone in the world but me. I will have to call you "Basso Profundo". On top of that, you're as stubborn as a mule!'

'That's because my family are Welsh originally but they all moved to London long before I was born. The Welsh are a stubborn lot.'

Bob didn't appear to take this in.

'I look upon you as a daughter,' he said.

* * *

My head gradually got better over the weeks when the toxins disappeared from my blood and the melancholy dispersed. I wasn't feeling well the first night in the Maxwells' house but Nicky's presence at dinner, combined with his joviality and quick humour, relieved me somewhat.

I soon settled down and there was no question of my parents enquiring about my whereabouts all this time as they assumed I was at college studying for my A levels.

The Maxwell children were all staying in the house and they were very friendly towards me. Isabel and Anne compared their lives with mine and we talked at length in the sauna about our respective contacts with the opposite sex.

From what I heard, Bob was very strict with his daughters and made a point of finding out whom they were seeing.

Isabel told me a rather bizarre story. She said she had told her father she was going to the Maxwell bookshop to have a look around. Incidentally, Bob had very kindly told me I could go there whenever I wanted and said I could put any purchase on his account.

Isabel went to the shop where she met a man who interested her. The man invited her downstairs where they had coffee and exchanged addresses.

When she returned home, Bob called her into his study.

'Was there something you wanted, Daddy?'

'Yes. Go over there and sit down.'

Isabel obeyed and asked what all this was in aid of.

'You said you were going to the bookshop to have a look around. You met a man there, didn't you?'

'Only by chance, Daddy.'

Bob looked at his teenage daughter sternly.

'I'm disappointed in you, Isabel. You have deceived your father.'

'That's a strange story,' I said, not knowing what else to say. I climbed down from the wooden benches to ladle more water on to the coals and poured more water over myself.

'Surely you couldn't have taken the incident too seriously,' I said. 'Perhaps your father was over-reacting a bit. Maybe he didn't quite understand what happened.'

'I felt dreadful about it for several months.'

'Several months? Several bloody months? You get over a trivial incident like that in 24 hours or 48 at the most.'

Isabel seemed annoyed.

'You don't understand, I felt my father couldn't trust me.'

'Nobody in the world trusts me but I don't get into a state for several months about it.'

'Was your father very strict with you?' she asked.

'Yes. He was kind but very stern. particularly if he was disobeyed. When I was about 8, he said: "Don't ever go down to the swimming-pool alone." I had just learnt to swim and I wondered why I wasn't to go there alone. I assumed there was something there that he didn't want me to see so I went there straight away when I thought he wasn't looking. Without my knowledge, he was doing some gardening nearby and he saw me coming back. I had a spanking but I was very brave, I didn't shed a tear.'

'If my father had told me not to do a thing, I would never have dreamt of doing it,' said Isabel. 'You sound as if you were really naughty. What else did you do?'

'I poured a bucket of gravel into my father's chauffeur's bowl of clean oil. My parents made me learn *The Charge of the Light Brigade* as a punishment. My mother even suggested I went to the chauffeur's house to recite it to him on his doorstep. My father said this wouldn't be fair on him because of my monotonous voice!'

Isabel and Anne, who had remained silent so far, roared with laughter and there's nothing I love more than an audience.

'Would you like me to recite it now?'

'I'd much rather you didn't,' said Isabel.

Isabel struck me as being by far the most serious of her siblings. Her identical twin sister, Christine, took life much more lightly. Isabel had a good sense of humour but somewhat quiet and reserved temperament. She was always gentle and kindly whenever I saw her.

She said: 'I'm afraid I've got to go now. I've got to get on with my essay. I'm due to read it to my tutor in the morning.'

I started talking to Anne.

'So what are you doing in life?'

This time it was her turn to ladle more water on to the coals.

'I'm going to be an actress. That is after I've got my degree. My father said I couldn't study drama before I've finished at University.'

'Your father strikes me as being quite strict with you all. Do you get on with him?'

Anne, who was shy, was taken aback by my question. I was sorry I asked it. She moved up to the top tier, saying how hot she was.

'I love my father very much and I'm proud of him and all the wonderful things he did during the war. It's true he's strict and can be unreasonable but he loves us all and bullies us into working like skivvies so that we can excel in life. Whenever I have a problem — provided of course it's not a lady's problem, if you see what I mean — he's really strong and supportive. The only person he's dotingly indulgent towards and spoils is Ghislaine.'

'Ghislaine? Who's she? I haven't met her yet.'

Anne came down again and watered the coals.

'Ghislaine's staying with a school friend. I don't know whether you know this but my brother, Michael, was in a coma following a road accident. We were very close. Ghislaine was born 3 days after Michael's accident in 1961. It was several years before Michael's life support machine was turned off.'

I was upset to hear all this.

'I'm so sorry. It must have been ghastly for you.'

'It was but as soon as Ghislaine was born we all felt she was a gift from Heaven. My father has always spoiled her. She gets away with more than we ever did. She's 9 now — 9 and naughty.'

Not long after I had settled in the house, I was fed up with my blonde hair. I decided to dye it black like Bob's and I wore it in a long plait, braided with ribbon to match whatever I wore. I was totally unaware of the fact that I looked like a middle-aged Chinaman.

I was afraid of dyeing it in the house in case I made a mess so I walked up the drive to the offices of Pergamon Press and dyed it in one of the washrooms there.

Bob was in his sombre study adjacent to his nice, light airy Empire living-room, looking at papers. I went over to him to kiss him as I always did the first time I saw him each day. He looked up and gave me a kiss on the mouth.

'My God, Ellie, why the hell have you done this to your hair?'

'I got fed up with being a blonde. I needed a change. Besides, women are always dyeing their hair.'

'But black doesn't suit you or your colouring. Your blonde hair was so lovely and you can't change nature.'

'Sorry, Bob,' I said. 'I'll wait till it grows out. I can't reverse it now.'

Ghislaine, the youngest, came into the room wearing blue jeans, tennis shoes and a white T-shirt. She clambered on to her father's knee and put her arms round his neck. He smothered her with loud smacking kisses.

'Who's that with you, Daddy?'

'That's not how one talks,' said Bob. 'One says: "My name's Ghislaine. I don't think I've met you before."'

Ghislaine repeated his words.

'I'm Eleanor. I'm a friend of your family. Nice to meet you.'

We shook hands.

'Why's your hair the same colour as Daddy's?'

'Don't be cheeky, Ghislaine,' said Bob but before he could get further I said, 'We both fell into the same inkpot. In other words, a silly question gets a silly answer.'

Ghislaine had been given a horse by her father. It was a time in her life when she loved horses before discovering men. The gate of the tennis court had been left open and her horse had wandered on to the court, leaving mounds of dung all over the place. It had also eaten its way through the net.

I was walking round the garden with Bob. We came to the tennis court. Ghislaine was lying on her back on the ground outside with her legs crossed, playing 'God Save the Queen' on a flute-like instrument known as a recorder.

'What's your horse doing on the tennis-court?' Bob asked mildly.

'I can't help it if some idiot leaves the gate open.'

Bob turned from subdued anger to merriment, caused by my hysterical giggles.

28

'It's not that I mind so much about your horse being on the tennis-court,' he said, 'but what I can't tolerate is its leaving its visiting card.'

I stayed talking to Ghislaine for some time. Though cheeky, there was a natural sweetness about her. She told me she was due to get a prearranged hiding from Bob that afternoon.

'You naughty girl! What did you do to irritate him?'

'Oh, I asked Judy and Jean to do a complicated job for me, without asking him.'

'Who are Judy and Jean and what did you ask them to do?'

'I told them to organize the transport of some horses — mine, and some friends' horses too. I told Judy and Jean — Judy Ennals and Jean Baddeley, two of Daddy's secretaries — to make arrangements for the horses to be taken to Basingstoke for a point-to-point, and returned to Oxford afterwards.'

I was quite surprised.

'Did these secretaries say they would carry out your orders?'

'Oh yes. I told them my father had said it was all right.'

'Well, did he?'

'No, of course not. You must be joking.'

I lit a cigarette in amazement. She asked me if she could have one too but I said no.

'You're very naughty, you know. How old are you?'

'Nine.'

'When you said your father was going to give you a "hiding" this afternoon, what sort of a hiding will it be?'

She looked nonplussed as if she thought she didn't deserve to be punished.

'Daddy has a series of things lined up in a row. There's a riding crop with a swish to it, another straight riding crop and a few shoehorns. He always asks me to choose which one I want.

'Well, which one will you choose?' I asked, fascinated.

'The shoehorn. That's the easiest.'

'What, for him or for you?'

'For me of course. If you were in my place, which one would you choose?'

By now, we were standing in a room adjacent to the Boardroom and I saw the various instruments of discipline in a row. I became peculiarly excited but hid this from her.

'I'd choose this one,' I said light-heartedly. 'The one with the swishing movement.'

'I waved it through the air and it made a noise as I went through the motions of striking an invisible object.

'Why would you choose that? It's the worst.'

I suddenly remembered I was talking to a child and was being irresponsible. I wondered what would happen if she told her father I had been discussing this sort of thing with her. She looked up at me, totally baffled.

'Why should you choose the one that hurts the most? I don't understand.'

I felt myself in check and got nervous.

'Because from what you told me, you've been very, very naughty. A 9 year old can't give orders to busy secretaries about horses. You should know better at your age, judging by all the trouble you've caused, and your punishment should fit the crime.

Had I behaved like that at your age, I would have been locked in my room and made to learn passages from Shakespeare by heart!'

Ghislaine seemed angry with me for not sympathizing with her.

'Would you like to be beaten by my father?' she shouted suddenly.

'I — I — I— er.' In other words I was struck dumb.

'Well, answer my question!' (She sounded just like her father).

'I don't give orders about horses to other people's secretaries. Nor do I respond to barked commands from 9 year- olds!' I said in mock anger. 'Does your father ride?'

'Not now he doesn't, but when he went fearlessly into battle, before getting his MC, flashing his sword in the shining sun, I feel sure he rode a horse!'

I suddenly felt very moved and endeared towards this pretty little girl with her pony tail and her father's lovely black eyes. I was terrified that she would steer the conversation back to the embarrassing subject I had no wish to discuss.

'When I went up the drive to your father's offices, I saw some puppies with one of the secretaries. They were so sweet,' I said guardedly.

She suddenly became animated.

'Yes. They're the puppies Tiger had. She and Whisky, our two labradors, had them together. Daddy often gives puppies to his secretaries. Some of the puppies are still in the basket with Mummy.'

'Where is the basket?'

'In the kitchen. Mummy's there now with Oping, preparing lunch.'

'Who's Oping?'

'Don't you know who Oping is? She's one of the Filipino ladies who help in the house.'

I went straight to the kitchen where I found Betty and Oping peeling potatoes. I greeted Betty and kissed her and introduced myself to Oping who had a cheerful, smiling face.

'So what have you been doing all the morning, Eléanore?'

'I've been in the sauna with Isabel and Anne. I went for a walk with Bob and I've been talking to Ghislaine.'

'Ghislaine?' said Betty. 'She's in disgrace with Bob and me. Her behaviour has been quite appalling.'

'Indeed? I heard from someone in the house that there had been some trouble in relation to horses.' I said vaguely.

'I don't want to talk about that. Come and keep me company.'

I helped her with the potato-peeling while she talked to me of love, literature, philosophy and life. What a magnificent mind she showed and what supreme sensitivity to art, music and beauty, and what a phenomenal and touching vision of the importance of the milk of human kindness. We spoke of Maupassant, Flaubert, Dostoevsky and Proust among countless other literary figures.

She knew the volumes of À la recherche du temps perdu intimately. Later at University, I had to study the latter work but confess with shame that I only read a synopsis of it in English just before my Finals.

'The most wonderful thing about Proust', she said 'is his preoccupation with the details the human mind sometimes misses. So many people take art and fortune for granted. Those with too much money, unable to put it to intelligent use, become idle and self-pitying. There are stockbrokers' wives forever sobbing into their gin and tonics, because they don't set themselves constructive occupational projects.'

I had to laugh when she said this. I tried to imagine what a gin and tonic would taste like laced with a discontented housewife's tears. I wondered if it would still be drinkable.

She peeled the last of the potatoes and Oping took them from her and put them in a boiling saucepan. She continued.

'Do you think that an empty-headed stockbroker's wife or a débutante would notice the things Proust noticed? I remember feeling very sad one day when the City were getting at Bob. I read one of Proust's tomes and found an intricate description of someone's balcony. Every inch of the fretwork was described in almost microscopic detail, even the shape of the beaks of the tiny bronze birds intertwined with the railings.'

I felt that if a human eye could be capable of remembering an object of beauty, just through walking past it, there would be no sadness in the world except in the hearts of the impoverished or the bereaved.

'Do you know Keats's poem which begins 'No, No! go not to Lethe?'

'I know the one you mean. I had to write an essay on it but I confess I don't know it by heart. In comparison with you I'm a dreadful philistine. When I go down, I don't go out and gape at the countryside, which doesn't do much for me anyway as I prefer to be surrounded by concrete buildings. I'm a Lethe man, myself. I go out and get pissed. That usually does the trick.'

She laughed. I was relieved not to have shocked her.

'You really are a one! That's what Bob likes about you so much.'

I loved Betty and I still do. In fact, since Bob's tragic death, about which I will speak later, I would be prepared to do anything in the world for her, because she is the very epitome of human perfection. She even got up early to drive me to the examination hall to help me to be more relaxed when I was doing my A levels in English, French and Russian before going to University. She would wait outside the hall and take me out to lunch to put me at my ease before doing my next examination. No one in the world would have done a thing like that and I shall remember it until the day I die.

'Ghislaine told me you had some puppies in here,' I said. 'May I see them?'

'Why, yes. They're over there.'

Six puppies, small enough to sleep in a man's shoe, played on a rug, surrounded by wire netting. Betty very kindly offered me one but I had to refuse it because my lifestyle would not have enabled me to look after it.

As we went back to the other part of the kitchen, I noticed a padlock on the larder door.

'What goes on behind that door?' I asked inquisitively.

'It's the larder. We have to lock it to keep Bob out when we put him on a diet; otherwise, he goes in and eats everything there is. He broke in only the other day as he's so strong he can break any door down. We had to change the lock. He's so naughty sometimes. Let's go next door and have a drink.'

The seven children were in the living room. Bob, who had been working all morning in the Pergamon offices, was standing behind the bar like a publican. He was in a good mood.

'What will you have, Missy?'

'White wine, please.'

'You'll be getting white wine at lunch. Have something stronger.'

32

'I'd like a gin and tonic, then.'

'Gin and tonic, it shall be.'

He gave me the glass and I took a few gulps. I felt a sense of euphoria as I stood there looking at Bob, feeling the warmth of the gin as it reached my stomach.

He came away from the bar and gave his familiar wolf- whistle.

'Come on everybody, let's go and have lunch.'

The children rose from their chairs immediately, as if responding to a formal command. Everybody took their seats at the table in the dining room overlooking the lawn. I sat on Bob's right and Jean Baddeley, his personal assistant, chief henchman and the only person in the world apart from his tyrannical father who was allowed to give him orders, sat on his left.

Food was passed round the table by one of the affable Filipinoes. I was hungry so I took more potatoes than I thought I needed. The dishes were passed to Bob who took an even larger amount of them.

Jean Baddeley turned furiously to the Filipino lady.

'I gave you specific instructions that Mr Maxwell was not to be offered potatoes!'

She took the spoon from the servant and shovelled the massive amount of potatoes off the wretched man's plate. To my surprise, he said absolutely nothing and I suddenly felt intensely jealous of the power Jean appeared to wield over him.

I picked up my own potatoes with my pudding spoon and put them on his plate.

'I wouldn't stand for that, Bob,' I said. 'Anyway, you're not fat so there's no need for you to be on a diet.'

He turned to face me and I noticed a profound look of love in his eyes.

'Oh, you are sweet!' he said.

After lunch, Isabel, who had always struck me as being the most serious member of the family, took me aside.

'Please don't do that again,' she said (very tactfully). 'Dad has a problem in relation to food and we all have to struggle to stop him harming himself.'

'What do you mean — harming himself? Why would potatoes harm someone?'

She lowered her voice as if about to break tragic news. I was getting increasingly confused.

'Once he starts eating carbohydrates, he just can't stop. Why else do you think we are locking him out of the larder at night? Do you know that he's only got one lung?'

'Yes.'

'The lung has to do the work of two. Extra strain is put on his heart with all this eating. Jean and I have to work really hard to keep him healthy, and today you undid precisely what we're trying to do.'

I couldn't understand what was going on. It was as if she were talking about a very elderly, ailing dog, not a 46-year-old hot-blooded, Samson-like Cossack.

At that time, Bob was well covered but not particularly fat. I decided the whole curious affair was none of my business.

'Sorry, Isabel, I won't do it again,' I said.

I stayed in the house for quite a few weeks. I was having breakfast with the family in the kitchen when the phone rang and Bob answered it.

My mother was on the line and asked to speak to me after speaking to Bob at some length. My mother asked why I had been away for so long. She said in short that I had been with the Maxwells for longer than the ethics of hospitality permitted and told me to come home. I went back to the table and sat down with Bob who had locked himself into his eating.

'Pamela (my mother) doesn't like you being in my house,' he said.

This statement carried a myriad of interpretations which it would be a bore to list.

I kept in touch with the family and saw them again within a few months when Bob asked me to come and work for him in his Buckinghamshire constituency on the 1970 election campaign.

He and his family occupied a very small but pleasant house overlooking a picturesque but stagnant canal. Jean Baddeley, who knew I was coming, organized a rigidly strict bath rota and had a long talk with me about the exact time I was to take a bath as well as its duration which was not to exceed 10 minutes.

These events coincided with an anti-airport rally in a town in Buckinghamshire organized by a then Tory barrister Desmond Fennell.

The Berrys had invited Bob, Fennell and his wife, Susan, to lunch before attending the rally and Bob gave me a lift. My siblings, Nicky and Harriet were there but Adrian was still covering a story in America. All I remember about this lunch is that Bob had been put on yet another diet by Jean Baddeley and Isabel, who had lectured him about the importance of keeping to his diet, with the result that he refused to eat anything except soup, as an alternative to being bossed about by two women.

Lunch was hurried and, afterwards, a number of cars set out from the house and steamed towards the rally. Mr Hoppitt, Bob's driver, said he knew the way. Bob stayed a while after the others had gone because he liked flowers and wanted me to show him the garden. There's nothing that bores me more than showing people round gardens about which I know nothing, but it was nice to see the delight Bob felt when looking at the flowers. He reminded me of Ferdinand the Bull.

'What are you doing with your life, Eleanore?' he asked suddenly.

'Studying languages.'

'Which ones?'

'French,' I said. My father was paying for me to do an extensive French course. I wanted to learn Russian but both my parents said I couldn't until I'd mastered French. Hence, I spent hours each day teaching myself Russian from tapes and grammar books and, because my will to learn it was so great, I had secretly become fluent in 6 months. I wasn't quite sure whether I should tell Bob my secret.

He had a conversation with me in French which appeared to meet with his satisfaction.

'Do you mean to tell me you only speak one language besides English?'

'No, I speak Russian too.' I told him my secret. He seemed peculiarly impressed. We had a long and even intimate conversation in Russian in which I expressed thoughts and told stories I would never have dared tell in English.

While this was going on, my father was looking for us. All the cars had left with the exception of my father's and Bob's Rolls-Royce occupied by Hoppitt, the chauffeur.

'Come on, Bob, it's time to go,' said my father.

'Hullo, Michael. God, you've got a smasher of a daughter! Look at her! I've never seen a girl like her in my life!'

'Oh indeed? For God's sake don't say that sort of thing in front of her. It will go to her head. Whose car are you going in?' he said to me.

'I'm going with Bob. We were having a fascinating conversation.'

'In that case, perhaps you'd care to get in and continue your fascinating conversation and ask the gentleman in your car to follow me.'

We spoke Russian for the whole journey. Hoppitt lost my father's car and neither of us had a clue how to get to the town where the rally was being held. It was evident that Bob did not have exactly the same burning interest in the airport as the others. He told Mr Hoppitt to stop outside a pub where we got out for a drink.

We arrived at the rally half an hour late because Hoppitt had been holding his map upside down until Bob indulged in his habit of hitting him on the head with a rolled up newspaper.

Apparently, as the rally had been going on for 15 minutes, my parents were asking agitatedly where Bob and I were. Nicky thought the whole situation amusing and Harriet raised her eyebrows in mischievous curiosity.

To get to the front row where my family were sitting, you had to walk down the aisle of a church-like building. Fennell, at the helm, stopped the speeches to wait for Bob.

He and I arrived. I was quite intoxicated by this time so I had to hold on to his arm. We were like a mad-looking couple of newly-weds except that we were continuing to speak animatedly to each other in Russian.

We sat on either side of my father behind my mother in the front row. We continued to speak Russian across my astounded father, regardless of the silence throughout the hall.

By this time my mother turned round, thinking we were making the words up.

'Aren't you impressed by the way Eleanore's taught herself Russian, without any help at all?' said Bob.

'I think it's absolutely extraordinary' said my mother. 'She's very clever to have done all that herself. You haven't been teaching her, have you?'

'No. It's obviously a gift.'

My father leant across Bob who was sitting with one leg crossed over the other at right angles.

'Come clean, Eleanor Berry. Why do you speak fluent Russian when we sent you out to perfect your French?'

Fennell banged the table for silence. He meant business and it was not his intention to fill the hall with the sound of Robert Maxwell and me booming at each other in Russian like a couple of foghorns.

Bob promised to send me the complete Pergamon Russian course. He kept his promise and 2 weeks later, a big crate, its contents worth over £300, arrived on my doorstep. It contained tapes and reproduced sections of Tolstoy as well as other Russian authors. Accompanied by this present, was a lovely letter from Bob.

Once in the Wharf House, working for Bob, Jean put us all on a bath rota. She had obviously remembered my habits when I first stayed with the family while I was recovering from my illness. Because of the severity of the disease, I took baths up to seven or eight times a day, laced with Dettol and pine essence and scoured my skin with a scrubbing brush saturated in Vim, in a pathetic attempt to wash the disease away. After this process I would empty the bath and fill it up with the same ingredients and start again, repeating the procedure three times.

Although there were a number of bathrooms at Headington Hill Hall, the one allocated to me was at the very top of the house and I shared it with the luckless Jean Baddeley, whose complaint that there was never any hot water for her and that the bathroom stank of disinfectant and Vim, as well as being permanently occupied, was not unjustified.

In the Wharf House there was only one bathroom.

'Mr Maxwell takes his bath at 5.00 a.m.,' said Jean strictly. 'Woe betide you if you're in there then.'

'OK, Jean, I won't be awake anyway at that hour.'

The rota didn't seem to work despite Jean's arduous organizing efforts. I went in one morning at 9.00 and got up to my usual habits which had not died although the disease had.

'Eléanore! What are you doing? Can you buck up?'

Betty needed to get in at the same time because the times of the rota had overlapped. This presented an ongoing problem. I arranged to take baths in the council house of a factory foreman called Nick who was also working for Bob.

At that time, I was still dyeing my hair black, which I did every two days and inadvertently blackened the foreman's towels. I didn't know what to do about this, whether to confess to the foreman and buy him a new set of towels or to say nothing. I decided to say nothing.

I tried another house belonging to another Maxwell worker but my reputation had radiated through the entire North Bucks Labour Party so the gentleman told me very politely to take my baths elsewhere.

The Maxwells had an Irish Charwoman whose name I can't remember but I have an idea it was Mrs Mock. I still had trouble getting up in the mornings. There was no clock in-time at the Party Headquarters so I wandered in whenever I felt like it. One of my duties was to wind the handle of a printing press producing huge photographs of Bob — this was by far my favourite job. I also had to sit in a row with a lot of jolly, ribald old ladies, passing documents down the line, stamping them, folding them up and putting them in envelopes.

I was happy in their company and in my surroundings. As we worked we cracked filthy jokes, each cruder than the one before. Bob came in and overheard us one day. He pushed our chairs with us still sitting on them, to separate tables scattered over the large hall, muttering something about lewd talk giving the Labour Party a bad name. Then he did the same to the chairs occupied by about ten other workers and pushed them, with the workers still sitting on them, to the table he'd taken us away from.

All this took him about 10 minutes. As he moved me over he said: 'You'll be pleased to hear I'm putting you next to a very good-looking man so be sure to keep your conversation nice and clean.'

'Forgive me, Bob,' I said sweetly, looking him straight in the eye with a seductive smile. He returned the smile.

'I'll forgive you but will the Almighty forgive you?'

The man I was put next to was a saucy fellow called Chris Brown. His conversation was even coarser than that of the old ladies. He had an essentially anal sense of humour and when Bob went back to his office, he talked about the various disciplinary departments in the sex shops he had visited.

'Chris, Bob said no lewd talk,' I said.

'It's all right now. He's in his office.'

I liked Chris Brown. We often went drinking together. He was always chatty and vivacious, but occasionally moody. He was neither cultured nor book-read but he nearly always had a joke to tell accompanied by an infectious laugh.

Sometimes, he took off my voice. This caused me a lot of conflict. Part of me thought how funny it was. The other part was irritated.

There were certain mornings when Bob did his paperwork in his study at the Wharf House. I knew he was in the house but I was still unable to get out of bed at a reasonable time. Besides, I thought he had far more important things to be doing other than checking when I got up.

Not so!

Mrs Mock, the charwoman knocked on my door at 10 a.m.

'Who's there?'

'It's Mrs Mock. May I come in?'

'I suppose so.'

She came in, looking as eccentric as ever. Her Irish accent was so thick, I could hardly hear what she was saying.

'Mr Maxwell says it's high time you were hopping out of your bed. He thinks you've been there quite long enough.'

'OK, Mrs Mock. I'll be up in a minute.'

She went away and I went back to sleep.

At 11 a.m. I was woken yet again by Mrs Mock.

'Mr Maxwell says it's high time you were hopping out of your bed. He thinks you've been there quite long enough. I came up an hour ago to tell you that and you're still there.'

The situation was repeated.

'OK, Mrs Mock. This time I will get up.'

'You'll have to get up now because Mr Maxwell wants me to come in and make the bed.'

* * *

The Labour Party canvassing van was an impressive sight covered with such slogans as *Harold and Bob will finish the job*. Mr Hoppitt, the family driver, was behind the wheel and Bob would stand up with his head and shoulders protruding through the roof talking through a megaphone.

'Vote when you can. Maxwell's yer man,' he would boom with hypnotic, if somewhat frequent repetition. 'Stop the van, Mr Hoppitt,' he said suddenly.

Hoppitt swerved in towards the pavement, on which a middle aged woman was walking with her dog.

'Morning, madam,' said Bob in a friendly tone. 'That charming basset of yours — what's his name?'

The woman turned round, looking inappropriately hostile.

'First, it's not a he, it's a she and it's not a basset, it's a Border terrier, and if you must know, it's name is Lucy.'

Bob looked piqued. 'Come on, Mr Hoppitt, let's go.'

Canvassing always took place in the evenings. I was prepared to do plenty of clerical work in the afternoons so I saw no immediate urgency in getting up early.

The family and secretaries assembled for lunch at a round table in a relatively small room. I sat next to Bob who turned to me straight away.

'There appear to be serious problems getting you up in the mornings. Do you realize the maid wasn't able to get in to make the bed?'

I started to get nervous giggles. There was something boyishly comical about his reprimand.

'It's not funny, Ellie. Tonight, I'm going to have you sleeping on a camp bed in my study.'

He started work in the study at 5.30 a.m. The bed was by the side of his huge desk so that he could see me. At 8.00 each morning, I was woken by his slow and deliberate, commanding baritone.

'Good morning, Eleanore.'

I ignored this and turned over. Two minutes later I was woken again.

'Wake up, Eleanore.'

I was still too drowsy to respond.

'Get up, Eleanore!'

I still ignored him. I was half asleep.

He got up and came to the bed and bent over me, his face almost touching mine. He jerked his thumb towards the ceiling.

'You! Up!'

An instinct told me the game was up for me. I obeyed.

I got used to sleeping in the study. Even at 5.30 a.m. he was making phone calls and I began to wake up much earlier. Sometimes when he thought I was still asleep, he would go through his papers. I would watch him in profile. Whenever he looked in my direction, I closed my eyes. It gave me so much pleasure to watch him at work when he didn't know he was being watched.

In the Headquarters, I met another, older man, also working for Bob. He was the Branch Secretary of a union and his name was Arthur Leary. He had a pleasant, gentle face framed by thick snow-white hair and he was devoted to Bob.

When I wasn't doing my favourite job, turning the handle of the printing press which, as well as Bob's photograph, churned out pamphlets called Maxwellgrams, I would work at a table with Chris Brown and Arthur Leary. We had to put stacks of envelopes into rubber bands and throw them into different baskets.

If I wasn't having lunch at the Wharf House, Chris, Arthur, Jean and I would go out to a restaurant. I have always had a voracious appetite for food and was never satisfied with what I ordered. I drank quite a lot which made me hungrier still and I leant over the table with my fork, taking things from Chris's, Arthur's and Jean's plates.

Arthur was half amused and half irritated. He marched me into Bob's office after lunch and spoke to him in a heavy Yorkshire brogue.

'Your little girlfriend tairks things from oother people's plairts!'

Bob looked disinterested.

'Don't worry about that, Arthur, I've taught her to take what she wants out of life,' he said.

I went canvassing that afternoon, accompanied by Betty and Ida, one of the old ladies who liked to crack coarse jokes. Ida was forthright and unusually talkative, like a washerwoman. Each time a bemused housewife answered the door, Ida would hurl a manic monologue expressing Bob's virtues to her.

I heard the shrill French voice of Betty who was sitting in the car.

'Ida! Come back to the car and get in!'

'Ida's not to canvass for me any more,' said Bob across the table to Betty at dinner.

'Who told you about Ida's canvassing?'

'Oh, just other canvassers.'

Up to now I had been going from house to house with Betty.

'I want Eleanore to go out alone,' said Bob. 'I think it would give her a lot of self-confidence and gain me a lot of votes.'

I felt very proud out there on my own with my pile of leaflets and the big pictures of Bob that I had printed on the machine myself.

I started on a line of red brick houses with neatly kept gardens.

'I'm canvassing on behalf of Robert Maxwell, the Labour candidate. Can we be counting on your support on Polling Day?'

The woman I faced was in her late 40s and wearing a neat brown dress. She came to the door knitting and went on knitting as I spoke to her.

'Sorry, dear,' she said with a smile, 'I'm a rabid Conservative.'

I got roughly the same reaction from the people behind the next few doors. I was getting bored and I thought of ticking off everyone on the list as being Tory, but I knew Bob wouldn't like that so I didn't.

The tenth house along was shabbier than the others and the garden was overgrown. I knocked on the door and said my spiel.

A man came to the door, in shirt sleeves, looking like a gangster from the pages of Sapper.

'Fuck off, you common little red tart!'

It was then that I made a monstrous mistake, one which I am embarrassed about to this day. I turned on my heels and ran home to Bob's house. I went straight into his study.

'Bob! A nasty man's just called me a little red tart.'

He looked up from his papers and stared me in the eye.

'Well, what did you do about that?' he asked, his head raised and his expression quizzical.

'I ran away,' I murmured.

He banged his hand (his left hand) down on the desk.

'I won't have to do with people who walk away like frightened dogs with their tails between their legs. We Maxwells don't do that sort of thing. We Maxwells are tough. I thought I'd tutored you well. Next time, you hit back. Do you understand?'

'Yes, Bob.'

I went out and got systematically drunk.

A few days later, I had an opportunity to prove to Bob I was not a coward. I had to canvass a street in a much rougher area. Most of its inhabitants told me they would be voting Labour. I came to a door, opened by a thin but muscular man with sandy-coloured hair and a torn white boiler suit. I could see a lot of rubbish in his hall and the banister on the facing staircase was about to fall off. I said my spiel again.

The man strode out of his house.

'So you're Labour, are you? It's because of this fucking Labour government that I've been out of work for 5 years!'

I didn't care what I said. I wanted the man to give me a black eye and rough me up a bit so that I could show my injuries off to Bob.

'It's not the government that's kept you out of work, you thug! You've been out of work because you're bloody incompetent.'

The man walked closer to me, his eyes full of hatred.

'Would you like me to beat you up and give you a good shag?'

I longed to walk into Bob's study covered in blood which would come off on his shirt when he greeted me. I wanted to be a heroine, an angel, a martyr and his henchman, wounded in the service of the King.

'I'd love that but I don't think you'd be capable of getting it up.'

I walked closer to him so that we were almost touching. I threw back my head and laughed like a streetwoman.

'Go on, hit me! I dare you. Why don't you try?'

'You ain't fucking worth it.'

He turned round and went indoors.

Jean happened to be canvassing the same street and had heard some of the dialogue between us. She looked flabbergasted.

'My God, I've never seen anything like it!' she said. 'I wouldn't have dared do that.'

She drove me back to the Wharf House. We both went into Bob's study for a drink.

'You should have seen Eleanore just now. I thought that man was going to kill her.'

'Come on, Basso Profundo, what happened? Let's have it!'

I told him the whole story leaving out my words about the man being unemployed because he was incompetent. I told him that the man had asked me if I wanted him to give me a 'good shag' and that I had told him I doubted he'd ever be able to 'get it up.'

Bob threw back his head and roared with laughter. How happy I was then! When he stopped laughing, he asked me a really bizarre question, still smiling.

'Were you very depressed afterwards?'

'Depressed!'

'Depressed.'

'No. Why should I be? I know I slipped up the other day but I like a socking good confrontation. It's like a gin and tonic.'

He gave me a very serious look and leant forwards in his chair.

'To do what you did then required a hell of a lot of courage. Do you know that?'

'I suppose so.'

'More courage than I've seen in anyone I know.'

The next few days, I was on a high. I worked hard, enjoying the company of my fellow workers and canvassing every evening.

Chris Brown and I were canvassing on opposite sides of a street in Newport-Pagnell, a sedate, neat and overtly xenophobic country village.

I walked up a tall, steep flight of steps, my hands full of leaflets and photographs of Bob and knocked on the door. The women I saw before me was about 60 and extraordinarily thin with a hollow face and hostile, staring beady eyes.

'I'm canvassing on behalf of Robert Maxwell, the Labour candidate. Can we be counting on your vote next Thursday?'

The woman stared at my eyes. I stared back at her until she averted her gaze. Suddenly, she formed her wizened hands into fists and for some unknown reason, started to pummel my hips with increasing ferocity.

'Get yourself and your stinking literature off my threshold!' Her accent wasn't local. She could well have been a colonial.

She seized my pictures of Bob from my hand and screwed them into a ball which she threw into the street.

I waited to see what she was going to do next and I didn't wait in vain. She continued to pummel me with her left hand and extended her right arm in a Nazi salute. I suspected I was dreaming this and would soon hear Bob's voice ordering me to get up.

The woman proceeded to sing the National Anthem. I waited for her to finish and only just managed to keep a straight face.

'You're bloody bonkers,' I said. 'Do you know that?'

The next thing I knew was that the maniac had pushed me down her steps. I felt something tear in my left arm as I fell. I realised I had done something to my wrist.

43

I was still holding the canvassing sheet. I took out my pen and with a trembling hand wrote against the woman's name. 'VERY DANGEROUS WOMAN!'

Chris Brown rushed over to me and helped me up. He looked at the canvassing sheet and my words beside the woman's name. He let out a guffaw. We stood there laughing like children. My arm was hurting like hell so Chris drove me back to the Wharf House.

Bob was in the kitchen, cooking scrambled eggs. He wasn't wearing a jacket and his tie was loosened at the neck with the top buttons of his shirt undone which set my blood on fire.

Chris had already told Jean what had happened. She rushed into the room.

'She was attacked, Mr Maxwell.'

'Attacked? Christ!' shouted Bob. 'Sit down and I'll bring you some scrambled eggs I've cooked.'

He brought two plates of scrambled eggs over to the table and sat down. I told him the story while he listened, fascinated. The scrambled eggs were cooked in butter and were good. It surprised me that Bob knew how to cook.

He was giving me a wonderful audience which made me forget the pain in my arm.

'So you say the batty old woman started hitting you?'

'Yes, that's right. This is what she did.'

I did the same to Bob as she had done to me. I hit his hips as she had done and I realized how cuddly he was. He threw back his head and laughed, looking me straight in the eye.

'Steady, Missy, you're beating me up!'

I did a demonstration of the woman singing the National Anthem as she saluted with one hand and went on hitting me with the other. I couldn't get the co-ordination right. My right hand mimicking the Nazi salute kept hitting Bob while my left hand didn't know whether to give the salute or do the hitting.

He was loving it. Suddenly, my injured left hand landed in the region of his liver. A terrible wave of pain went through me and I shrieked out loud.

'You hurt your arm when she pushed you didn't you, Missy?'

'Yes,' I said.

Bob put two fingers of each hand into his mouth and whistled. Jean came in.

'I do wish you'd stop that whistling, Mr Maxwell, every time you need attention. It's dreadfully common.'

'It's what they do at football grounds, isn't it?'

'What do you want, Mr Maxwell?'

'Get a doctor, please. I think Eleanore may have broken her arm.'

I went canvassing with my arm in a sling with Chris Brown again the next evening in an equally xenophobic country village.

I knocked on a door which was opened by an unshaven drunk and said my spiel. The man supported himself on the open door of his house and looked at me through watery red eyes, exhaling the smell of stale beer.

'I don't vote for crooks!' he said.

I lost my temper.

'Your words constitute slander in the first degree and they will be written down. Written down, I tell you.'

The man tried to slam the door in my face but I rammed my foot in just in time.

'What you really resent about this man is that he started with less than you and got further. You're a petty-minded provincial oaf.'

'The man swayed backwards and forwards as if about to fall. I heard Chris's voice behind me.

'Leave him, now. Just mark "no" on the canvass sheet and move on. Don't get into any arguments.

Two days later, Bob called me into his office.

'What is it, Bob?'

He was looking as serious as a High Court Judge. I was terrified he was going to notify me of an illness or a bereavement.

'What's happened, Bob?'

He came to the point without preamble.

'Eleanore! You are NOT to frighten my constituents.'

'I haven't frightened anyone! What are you talking about? Whom have I frightened?'

Bob cleared his throat, sounding like a gang of Hell's angels trying to start their motor bikes.

'We all know about this,' he said. 'There's something about the way you approach people that terrifies them.'

'But it was you who taught me to do that. That's why I do it and I don't even know I'm doing it.'

'Yes, I understand that. Frighten anyone you want but not in my bloody constituency. I'm trying to win this Election for Christ's sake!'

'All right, Bob. I won't do it again, I promise.'

'It's all right. I know your heart's in the right place but as of tomorrow, I'll have to send Philip to go round with you.'

Philip, one of my favourite Maxwell children, was and still is sweet, quiet, humorous and gentle. He had not inherited his father's looks and resembled his paternal grandfather.

As we got out of the car to cover a street, he said: 'Whatever you do, don't shout at anyone, Ellie. You may come across some ghastly old fart but be sure to be as polite as you possibly can.'

'No problem, Philip. Your father gave me a talking to last night.'

'I can well imagine he did! He sometimes tends to be the pot that calls the kettle black, if you'll pardon the cliché, but I love the old bastard all the same.'

Betty and I sometimes canvassed together. We had always shared an interest in the works of the Marquis de Sade.

We took a break and sat down on a seat in a neat, tidy village street and had coffee from a flask she had brought with her.

A heated, but friendly argument ensued between us about whether the 1787 edition of *Justine* had more or fewer merits than the 1797 edition. She agreed that the 1787 edition was better because of its theme that virtue is always rewarded and vice punished. I did not adhere to this view. I said that whatever virtue is committed, it achieves nothing.

One of the workers came up to us, leaning out of the campaign van, reminding us that lunch was at 1 and that it was now 1.30.

'Are you both all right?' asked the worker.

'Yes, perfectly,' said Betty. 'We were arguing about a Frenchman.'

* * *

I was standing in an idyllic village square with Chris and Arthur among a crowd. The scenario could have belonged to the eighteenth century. Creepers hung in abundance from the walls of a pub, outside which I saw three brawny, over-nourished, xenophobic- looking, shabby, cloth-capped rustics sitting with their backs to the crowd, their braces so tight they looked as if they were about to snap. They were swigging from great big brimming beakers of Newcastle brown ale and stuffing themselves with fish and chips.

They ate and drank in a gross and bestial manner, so engrossed in pumping rubbish into their stomachs that they didn't speak to each other although they appeared friends.

Looking at them, I formed an immediate opinion that they weren't very nice.

46

Bob's campaign van, driven by the phlegmatic Mr Hoppitt, pulled up in front of the crowd. The date was 10th June and Bob's supporters sang 'Happy Birthday' which appeared to irritate and embarrass him. Bob leant out of the roof of the van and addressed his flock, speaking as usual about pay rises, corrupt landlords persecuting the working classes, schools, tied cottages and all that sort of stuff.

I noticed the three sinister-looking rustics by now full of beer, advancing with staggering gaits towards the crowd. Instinctively, I picked up a stick and moved through the crowd in their direction. I could tell they meant harm.

One of them, a white-haired old man interrupted the speech at a point where Bob was making a joke, a very bad one, I admit, but a joke nevertheless.

'It's lucky there's a fish and chip shop next to the pub, isn't it?'

'You wouldn't be standing up there like that if you'd been able to buy the *News of the World*,' said the white-haired rustic.

'I don't think this is an occasion to be personal,' said Bob, I thought amazingly mildly.

The man pursued his quarry. I moved towards the white-haired rustic clutching my stick.

'How can you call yourself a socialist if you have a Rolls Royce and trusts for your children in Liechtenstein?'

Bob lost his temper.

'Your words are utterly slanderous and you are deliberately instigating a smear campaign against me!'

I raised the stick holding it behind my head to hit the man. I was about to bring it down on him.

'Eleanore, don't hit him!' shouted Bob. I was so startled that I dropped the stick. I took three paces backwards and lowered my head.

The somewhat alarming news transpired during the campaign that Bob's agent, a left-winger called Jim Lyons, had a grudge against him. It was said that he failed to do the administrative work required of him and apparently hassled his pro-Bob deputy agent whose name, I think, was Bill Turner.

Turner was devoted to Bob but suffered from a severe, ongoing mental illness apparently exacerbated somewhat by Lyons's alleged insensitivities. Turner tried to tell Bob what he rightly or wrongly thought was going on and referred to his mental illness. His methods of expressing his thoughts were muddled and incoherent with the result that Bob became very impatient. He had had no idea what he was talking about and ignored him.

Lyons was now alone in the campaign van which he had allowed to run out of petrol in a quiet village street. The loudspeakers were turned on and Lyons started swearing his head off. Four-letter words blasted round the Labour Party Headquarters' loudspeakers like confetti.

Arthur Leary took command of the situation and rushed over to the microphone, aware that Lyons's obscene tirade was reverberating all over the constituency.

'Watch the language you're using! Over.'

'I'll use what bloody language I want. I'm out of fuel.'

'I'll tell the Boss,' said Arthur assertively.

'Tell anyone you sodding well like. You know what I think of that bastard!'

Bob came in after all this had happened.

'Where the hell's Lyons, Arthur?'

'His van's broken down in a village street. He's out of fuel.'

'Bloody fool! Where the hell's Bill Turner?'

'I'm afraid he's had to go to a psychiatrist.'

'Why?'

'Because he said Lyons had driven him off his head.'

'Why didn't he come to me?'

'He did but you weren't able to understand a word he said.'

'In that case, I don't think the psychiatrist will either.'

Arthur smiled politely and hinted to Bob what he thought Lyons was up to.

'I'm not too confident we're going to win this f***ing election, Arthur.'

Bob was doing his 'surgery' the next day. An agitated woman brought her daughter, a waif-like creature aged about 15 into his office and told him she was pregnant. She asked him what she should do about it.

Bob addressed his questions to the girl rather than her mother.

'Why don't you marry the child's father, settle down and make a go of it?'

'I couldn't do that,' said the girl.

'Why not?'

'Because I don't know who the father is.'

'Why don't you know who the father is?' asked Bob, getting bored and impatient.

'Well, it could be one of five. It could be Eric, John, Martin, Ned or Ken. It was a Saturday night and I had a gang bang.'

Bob looked aghast.

'Blimey, madam, you really have put my king in check!' was all he could think of saying.

This legendary story travelled all over the constituency, at the speed of light. It was told, with increasing exaggeration in pubs, cafés, among cinema audiences and many other places. It even got into the local paper.

Ida, the noisiest woman in the workforce, was always accompanied by her elderly mother who also made a hell of a lot of noise but wasn't as noisy as her daughter. Ida's maternal grandfather came to the Headquarters every day. He looked about 110 and the only reason for his permanent presence was that there was nobody at home to look after him.

He would occupy a chair in the middle of the room and slump with his head thrown back, his eyes closed and his toothless mouth gaping open. People seeing him for the first time assumed automatically that he was dead and quite a few women screamed.

Sometimes, Bob would resurrect the situation by walking past this man, ruffling up his snow-white hair and patting him on the shoulder, muttering, 'How yer doing, Grandpa?'

Betty was terrified of the man.

'Do we have to have him in here, Bob? He gives me the creeps. "Is he dead?" I keep asking myself.'

'Don't be stupid! He's got nowhere else to go. Why shouldn't we have him here? He's not doing anyone any harm.'

'But, Papa (she often called him that), he seems in perpetual rigor. It makes the place look like a mortuary.'

'I've told you he can stay so that's it.'

'Is there any reason why he can't sit in your office?'

Bob got irritated.

'I don't want him in my bloody office!' he bellowed.

The workers were used to assuming the old man was more likely to be dead than alive and he got accepted as part of the furniture.

It was during Bob's passionate, famous Eve of Polls speech when cameras clicked and flashed around him, making me indescribably excited, that it became apparent, on account of a somewhat disagreeable odour, that the old man had indeed died. In fact, he'd been dead for some time and even Bob, with his repeated hair ruffling and 'How yer doing, Grandpa?' had no knowledge that he was talking to a stiff.

A small amount of scuffling took place around the man. Bob's speech was over after tumultuous applause and supporters began to shuffle out.

49

A neat-looking man mounted the platform and gave Bob a note. He read it and looked surprised.

'I think one ought to generally send for a doctor, he said.

'A bloomin' 'earse, more likely!' shouted a supporter.

When the agitated workers gathered at the Wharf House, and as women clucked in clattering manic voices, I could hold out no longer. The whole situation had turned into a macabre farce. I was absolutely convulsed with giggles. The tears poured down my cheeks and the attack was so bad I couldn't even stand up.

'What's the matter, Eléanore?' asked Betty, looking very concerned.

'Menstrual cramps. I'll go outside in the fresh air.'

'Has she got a temperature, Betty?' Bob's voice boomed from the other side of the room.

'No' No' Papa,' adding very quietly, 'Just the usual.'

Horrendously embarrassed, I staggered outside and lay on my stomach by the canal, waiting for the giggling attack to subside.

Attention had turned from stiffs to polls. I came back and saw Bob in the hall.

'Feeling better, Eleanore?'

'I feel fine.'

I gave him a kiss and said: 'Good luck, Bob.'

'I may need it. Most people round here think I'm a bloody Bolshevik.'

The problem regarding baths was recurrent. I decided to take one at 3 a.m. I went through the usual procedure of filling the bath with Dettol and foam and lay there.

The handle on the door was turned with furious persistence. I ignored it.

'Philip, what the f***ing hell are you doing in there?' bellowed Bob.

'It's not Philip. It's Eleanor.'

'All right. I'll be back in three quarters of an hour.' (He sounded pissed off).

Polling Day dragged on exhaustively. I got on a train to London where I voted Tory in my own constituency because I felt like it at the time. Even so, I desperately wanted Bob to win in his constituency so I took another train back to Milton Keynes, picked up my brother's car at the station (I'd smashed my own car up while listening to Beethoven's Ninth) and drove Labour Party supporters to the Polls.

My behaviour that day made me feel pretty odd. My right hand has never known what my left hand was doing. I felt sweaty and disorientated but I knocked back a socking great gin and tonic after the Polls had closed and felt fractionally more normal.

It was on the cards, due to the Mori polls, that Labour would win on a landslide. I went into Bob's study accompanied by the whole family, Chris, Jean, Arthur and one or two other campaign workers.

Bob sat with his feet on the desk, with the top two buttons of his shirt undone and his tie loosened. My eyes were more often focused on him than on the television.

After about an hour, it transpired that Labour were losing. Bob muttered the word 'Christ!' a few times. Most of his family looked downcast, particularly Betty, and a few of the women were in tears.

When Bob's friend, George Brown lost his constituency and posed before cameras looking as if all his relatives had been run over by a tram, there was a deadly silence in the room and even Bob, who incidentally always cried very easily when sad, looked close to tears on watching his friend's grief.

The hush in the room was interrupted by a disastrously tactless remark from Ian, one of Bob's sons, then aged about 13, to his sister, Isabel who was sitting on the floor by his side. Ian is a delightful person but there have been some few occasions in his younger life when he has offered the putter to someon whose ball was still in the bunker.

'What do you think, Izzy?' he said, his commanding voice raised. 'When it comes to Dad's beat, he'll lose by the skin of his teeth after a couple of recounts? Let's bet on it, Izzy.'

At least Isabel didn't reply and lowered her head. Bob looked away from the screen and focused his piercing gaze on his son.

'Ian, if I were you, I'd watch it or you're going to be sorry. You know what that means, don't you?' he said in an ominous tone.

I assumed this meant the promise of a thrashing and I started to breathe heavily. This was caused partly by my having been turned on and partly because of my secret shame that I had sneaked off to London and voted Tory.

The craggy face of Reginald Bosanquet filled the screen. He has never struck me as being a particularly good-looking man but Anne, the only blonde in the family then an actress and the oldest survivor of the Maxwell children, evidently liked the look of him and tried to cheer the gloomy atmosphere in the room. She mimicked a perfect cockney accent.

''Ullo, dearie! Fancy a roll in the 'ay darlin'? Don't squeeze the fruit unless yer wants to buy it!'

Her spontaneous effort to provide comic relief had a profoundly irritating effect on Bob, either because he may have considered her outburst vulgar or because he failed to see there is a funny side to all things grave, or both. He lost his temper.

'For Christ's sake, shut up! I can't hear a bloody thing when you're cracking dirty jokes. One more sound out of you and I'll take you upstairs and tan your backside, as big as you are!'

These two threats of the infliction of corporal punishment by the hand of this hunky male sex siren were more than I could handle. The lust they inspired in me caused me to hyperventilate. I had to go upstairs and immerse myself in a stone-cold bath for half an hour. I returned to the study, assuming my absence was unnoticed.

'Where the hell have you been, Eleanore?' boomed Bob in his magenta velvet baritone, his tone half angry. 'Surely you couldn't have taken yet another bath? Jean says you've had two already today.'

'I didn't take a bath. I'm finding the news so awful I went out to get some air, that's all.'

He raised his head, his face in repose which he always did when he knew he was being lied to, but because the incident was trivial, he decided to let it ride.

We stayed up until 4 a.m. by which time we knew the Tories were going to win by a landslide. Bob sat, supporting his face with his hands. It was possible he may have been hiding his tears. The count in his constituency would not be taking place until late that morning. We were all exhausted and shuffled despondently out of the study.

I was the last one to leave. I began to walk slowly across the room with my head lowered.

I felt someone behind me running their fingers through my hair and winding it in a circle. I turned round and saw that it was Bob. He put his arm round my neck and kissed me on the cheek.

'Thank you so much, Ellie.'

'But I failed,' I said, very close to tears.

Chris, at Bob's side, said: 'She's been a bloody brave canvasser.'

'Yes,' said Bob, 'she's got nerves of steel and her heart's in the right place; there's no doubt about that.'

The three of us had a drink which diminished our gloom. Bob said: 'It's a full house tonight, I'm afraid, so you'll have to share a room with Bill Turner. There's a bunk there. There's no need to worry about him making advances, though. He's queer.'

Bob gave me a bear hug before we went to our respective beds. I found Bill Turner lying face down on the top bunk, sobbing his guts out.

I really can't handle it when men cry and I stood there staring at him. At length, I managed to drag out some well-meaning but ill-chosen words.

'Why do you have to take these things so hard, Bill? There'll be another election in 5 years and another 5 years after that. Besides, you did your best.'

'It's not that. It's that man, Jim.'

'Do you mean Jim Callaghan? I don't understand you.'

'No, Jim Lyons. He hates poor Bob.'

I was exhausted and didn't particularly want to hear anymore about the unsatisfactory relations between Jim Lyons and Bill Turner.

'You shouldn't have let him get to you,' I said impatiently. 'If a man ruffles another man, the ruffled man should beat the culprit up, instead of crying about it.'

Bill didn't answer. I got into the lower bunk. Although I sympathized, I wasn't interested in his problems which depressed me. My main concern was that I might talk in my sleep and reveal my terrible secret that I had gone to London to vote Tory. I stuffed my mouth with tissue paper to prevent any movement of my tongue and gagged myself with a scarf.

When Betty came in to wake me, she was baffled by my appearance. I muttered something about fear of talking in my sleep and upsetting Bill by shouting foul language and she took it as a joke.

We all set off in a convoy of cars and vans, not unlike a funeral procession, in the direction of the Town Hall where the count was taking place.

All Bob's supporters, including myself flocked into the market place outside the Hall. The gathering was rowdy and some sections of the crowd were angry, bitter and vicious. I have always had a *tricoteuse's* mentality and I get carried away on the wave of mass hysteria. I edged over to the angry section and reached a climax of rage for Bob's sake and his tears if not for the sake of the Labour Party.

I was getting more and more manic. I slid into an Irish accent to betray my origins and started shouting, 'Kill! Kill! Kill!' The crowd around me followed my lead.

A rough, attractive-looking, well-built man, whose name I had forgotten but whom I had spoken to on a number of occasions before, flashed a jagged-toothed grin at me and knelt on the ground, brandishing a huge home-made red flag with an intricately-embroidered hammer and sickle on it.

'Come on, El, get on my shoulders and wave the flag!

I took a strong liking to this man and got on his shoulders. He forced his way to the front of the crowd with me on top of him, waving the flag in circles round my head like a maniac. It gave me pleasure to be on a pedestal above the throng, flaunting myself in honour of my hero and idol.

The man carrying me lifted me to the ground immediately outside the Town Hall. From a flag pole at the top of the building, the Union Jack billowed in the fresh June wind.

'Go on, El,' said the man, 'there's a fire-escape at the back of the building. Shin up it, take the Union Jack down and put the red flag in its place.'

I have always been singularly unfit because I hate taking physical exercise. The idea of 'shinning' up a metal ladder, carrying a red flag, was somewhat daunting but it was not a challenge I was prepared to refuse.

I gripped the thin flag pole between my teeth and began to mount the ladder, without looking down. It was a surge of mania alone, combined with self-glorification because I naively felt I was making history, that drove me to the top. I was drunk on my own megalomania, feeling at that moment that Bob's and my souls were united. I recited the first few verses of *Horatius* to myself and finally dragged myself on to the roof.

I made my way towards the Union Jack. I lifted it from its berth and threw it over the edge of the building, just missing the cheering crowd who descended on it like vultures and ripped it to pieces as they chanted and cheered.

I carried the red flag in my right hand and walked backwards and forwards along the roof, waving it in the air imagining I was Lawrence of Arabia flouncing on top of the train, and Isadora Duncan dancing the *Slav March*, in rhythm to the rousing revolutionary songs sung by my admirers.

'Put up the flag, comrade! Put up the flag!'

I did as I was told. I put the flag where the Union Jack had been. The crowd started to sing 'The Internationale'.

I'm afraid my pleasure was short-lived. I heard a loud voice with a local accent bellowing up at me from a loud hailer. It was a policeman.

'Eleanor Berry, will you please remove that flag and come down to the market-place.'

I made the mistake of walking right to the edge of the building. A horrible attack of my recurrent vertigo took me over. It seemed as if the building had turned itself on its side and I thought I was about to fall off it. Everything around me was spinning and I suffered from mounting nausea. I lay on my stomach, hoping the building wouldn't tilt any further.

'I told you to come down to the market-place, Eleanor Berry, bringing that flag with you,' said the policeman, 'and if you fail to obey my orders you will be brought down by force.'

I was not aware at the time of what was going on below. I was told later that someone in the crowd had given the policeman the following advice.

'She won't respond to your orders, Officer. There's only one person with the power to get her down and that's Mr Maxwell inside.'

A few minutes later, I heard Bob's voice coming from the loud hailer. He had come out of the building by which time he knew he had lost his seat to the nondescript Tory candidate, Bill Benyon.

'Ellie!'

I didn't answer because of the vertigo.

'Eleanore! Will you please do what the Police are telling you to do. Take down the red flag and stop being so naughty!'

'I'll try to come down Bob, but I've got very bad vertigo,' I shouted.

'If you get vertigo, you shouldn't have gone up there in the first place. Will you please come down?'

I obeyed him as well as I could but I couldn't find the ladder. I noticed two policemen coming on to the roof.

'Why didn't you make any effort to come down when I spoke to you?' said one.

'I've got vertigo. I can't walk but you can carry me if you wish.'

The other policeman removed the red flag and threw it to the ground where the bottom of the ladder was. The first one gave me a fireman's lift which must have looked singularly undignified. It was fortunate that the ladder was at the side of the building and out of the crowd's eyeshot. My vertigo disappeared once I was on the ground. I went round to the front where the crowd broke into spontaneous cheering.

Bob came out of the building again, looking sad and dejected. He got into the canvassing van. I tried to cheer him up by waving the salvaged red flag outside. He smiled. Then he spoke to his supporters through the loud hailer in the van.

'Thank-you all for your courageous and loyal support. We are disappointed but not downhearted. We have lost a battle but not the war.'

Ida and her mother, near the front, roused the crowd into singing *For he's a Jolly Good Fellow.* I got into the van where Betty was sitting in the passenger seat. Arthur Leary, Chris, Jean and Bob's son Kevin, then about 10, sat in the back. I joined them and we returned to the Wharf House to clear everything out.

Betty and I did this together. I asked her, as delicately as possible, if I could take two of Bob's shirts from the bedroom drawer. She handed them to me unquestioningly. I still have these shirts with their sleeves extending nearly a yard over my hands and I use them as night dresses and sometimes during the day to give me confidence regardless of my ridiculous appearance.

The clearing out process took about 2 hours. Then the van was driven down Labour supporting streets with Bob standing up saying 'We have lost a battle but not the war.' Chris Brown was driving. I sat between him and Arthur. Bob sat behind us holding my hair and explained he was doing this because there were no seat belts in the back.

Despite the defeat, I was supremely happy during this journey, being surrounded by men with my favourite one holding my hair. Chris saw two Tories walking down the street, wearing blue rosettes and laughing. He wound down the window and leant out.

'Bloody Tories! Let it drop in and pull the chain!'

Bob said nothing but when I looked at him through the driver's mirror, I saw he was smiling.

We returned to the Wharf House for lunch. We went into Bob's study for drinks and found Bill Turner sitting there weeping. He rose to his feet and walked over to Bob.

'I'm so ashamed, Bob of failing to stand up to Jim Lyons.'

Bob ruffled the weeping man's hair.

'It's all right, Bill. It's all right.'

But as he left the study to go into the dining room, I could see from his face that he regarded Turner with pathos and disrespect for his lack of courage.

'That poor man!' I said, turning to Bob. 'It's clear how much he admires you.'

'I understand that but he's a bit gaga.'

The lunch was a very sad occasion. Ida and her mother had tears in their eyes throughout the meal. Betty's voice was sad and flattened. Bob said very little but cheered up when beer was provided for him.

There was a moment of comic relief when a rich-looking home-made chocolate cake was brought into the room. Ghislaine leant across the table and licked it. Betty ticked her off but Bob was unable to keep a straight face when he saw his favourite child who could do no wrong at that stage in her life, being tiresome.

The family and I left the house after lunch and returned in a convoy of cars to Headington Hill Hall. I travelled alone with Bob in the campaign van and during the one and a half hours it took to drive from Milton-Keynes to Oxford, I had the longest conversation with him in my life.

He was a very fast, impatient but good driver. Every time he had to come to an abrupt halt, he thrust his outstretched left arm in front of me as the van was not fitted with seat belts.

'Does Michael (my father) ever get angry or jealous of me and my relationship with you?' he asked suddenly.

'If he does, I've never heard anything about it. Do you think it annoys him?'

'Yes.'

'Why?'

'Because I would resent it in his position. If he were to take the same interest in Isabel, I'd go round to see him and put a stop to it.'

'A stop to what?'

'A stop to the friendship, of course. I'd get suspicious because I'd have no idea what it would lead to.'

'My father's not suspicious,' I said. 'He's got nothing to be suspicious about.'

Bob ruffled my hair and laughed like a Cossack.

'That's right,' he said. This was an expression he always used when he was getting bored with a topic of conversation. He always laid the emphasis on the word 'right.'

A short silence ensued, broken by Bob.

'Are you still seeing all those f***ing doctors? Why did you get involved with all those psychiatrists? What went wrong?'

I told him the entire story and the only details I left out were those he knew already. Strangely, he did not appear bored and listened throughout, only interrupting me occasionally.

'So you were very shielded when you were little, no doubt because you were the youngest.'

I also told him that I had had a morbid and pathological fascination for Russian literature during adolescence. I said my obsession about it was so extreme that I could think of nothing else during my waking hours and that in short, it haunted me.

'It haunted you. Why?'

To give an example, I described Gorki's *Foma Gordyev*. It took me 15 minutes and Bob, who was always noted for his extreme impatience, still did not interrupt me. The book is centralized on industrial relations in the timber transport industry and a wealthy man's barges travelling up and down the Volga in nineteenth-century Russia. I didn't describe it in this way because I was terrified that Bob might fall asleep at the wheel and drive into a ditch.

Instead, I told him it was about a boy, an only child who had been spoiled by his drunken father who was the then equivalent of a millionaire and the owner of a considerable number of barges combing the Volga. I said relations between him and his underlings were poor.

I saw from the corner of my eye that Bob was looking puzzled, but still he didn't interrupt me. Indeed, he gave me a far more intelligent audience than any psychiatrist I'd seen.

I didn't realize this at the time but I was in fact shouting hysterically at this man who, like Roderick Usher losing his sister, had just lost the seat which, apart from his family, meant almost everything to him.

I continued to describe the boy's father entering his son's room at dawn to say he was dying and that he needed tea outside under the apple trees and a priest to be summoned immediately. I mentioned that apples fell into the tea just before the father expired.

For the rest of his life, the boy was lost without his father, and his bereavement, accompanied by his inability to get on with his greedy contemporaries caused him to become insane. His fellow merchants didn't know what to do so they tied him up and sent for his godfather.

'Christ! When the hell's this story going to end?' shouted Bob who had been courteously silent up to now.

'It ends this way....'

Bob interrupted me.

'There's no need to shout. I can hear you perfectly well.'

'It ends this way,' I repeated again in a quieter tone. 'The boy, now a man, who never recovered from his father's death, went more and more insane until he was put into a lunatic asylum.'

'Had you lost someone you loved very much?' asked Bob. 'Were you identifying yourself with the man in the book?'

'No that didn't happen at all. Have you read it?'

'Yes, I read *Foma Gordyev* just after the War. I'm bound to say you didn't advertise it very interestingly. I think I know what it was about it which hit you so hard. It was its profound purity, richness of language and use of metaphor. You loved the book so much that I bet you read it over and over again and each time you found even further evidence of purity. In fact, you saw so much purity that you were disillusioned that no such purity existed in what you saw of life. You couldn't reconcile yourself to reality after seeing a fantasy world in the form of stirring and beautiful language, because there was no pleasure in your life when you read it. Did you read it in Russian?'

'Good God, no! In English. My Russian's not up to reading a book like that.'

'You've got looks, guts, brilliance, loyalty and wit. You're a very attractive girl. Have you ever thought of getting married?'

'I haven't found the right man, yet.'

'To get married you must love the man you're marrying and he must love you. In life there are those who give and those who take. To which category do you belong?'

I gave him an honest answer.

'Naturally, I prefer to take than to give but on all occasions when I have taken, I always go out of my way to give in return. That's how I feel about you. I took so much from you and you gave without motives. That's the reason I will do anything for you in return.'

'Will you do one thing, then?'

'What?'

'You're shouting again. Just talk in an ordinary voice. I'll hear you.'

For some totally unknown reason, I started talking about Henry II and his quarrel with Becket. Perhaps I was thinking of Bob putting those he thought he could trust in high places and being betrayed by them, but because Bob appeared neither familiar with Henry II nor Becket, the topic was short lived.

The rest of the conversation took place in Russian. By the time we got to Headington Hill Hall, Bob whose eardrums must have been perforated by my manic shouting, was exhausted and slept until dinner.

Ghislaine came up to me in the hall and pointed to her suitcase.

'Will you take this up to my room, please,' she said.

'No, I will not. I'm not your maid.'

'Will you come up and push me on my rocking horse?'

'I'll certainly do that if it's what you want.'

While I was pushing her she said suddenly.

'I don't think you're Labour at all. I think you're a Tory.'

'Why?'

'I've just heard things, that's all. I know you went to London on the day of the Election and I have reason to believe you voted Conservative.'

'You can have reason to believe anything you want.'

'Just tell me. I won't repeat it. Did you vote Conservative?'

'No. Anyway, it's time for dinner.'

Kevin had already come into the room to say dinner had started. He even briefed me on what was being discussed at dinner. He had about him a clinical formality in the manner he spoke accompanied by quite a dry sense of humour. He was intellectually advanced for a 10 year-old child, sharp, intuitive and concise. I couldn't make him out. Also, he got rather cross at breakfast the next morning because there were no Rice Crispies.

'You're late,' said Bob as I sat down in the vacant chair on his left.

'Yes, I know. Ghislaine wanted me to play with her in her bedroom.'

'It is not Ghislaine who gives the orders in this house. It's her father,' said Bob.

I could tell instantly that he was feeling depressed.

'I'm sorry, Bob. I promise I won't be late again.'

As I spoke I stared at his eyes. That way, I got a smile out of him. Ghislaine walked round to him and asked him to pull a wishbone with her. She got the wish and he asked her what it was.

'I made a wish that you would win next time,' she said.

He took her on his knee and caressed her. This made me irrationally jealous.

When Bob was subdued, it was not uncommon for his children to be infected by his mood. Sometimes, he would break the silence by putting very sudden questions to anyone around him. On a few occasions I was the recipient of one of these questions but I always barked at him and that seemed to make him laugh.

Jean, sitting on Bob's right, made some comment about the Common Market, implying that she favoured the country's integration into a united Europe.

Bob turned to me.

'Eleanore, does that support your view?'

'No, it doesn't. By that criteria, a nation is robbed of its individuality and it becomes a mere county within a massive soulless state.' (I realized I was shouting again.)

Bob looked a bit startled by my tone of voice and then he suddenly laughed.

There was an interval in the conversation. The children talked among themselves for a while until Betty entered the conversation.

'What are we going to do about that heinous Jim Lyons, Papa? Not only has he lost you your seat through sheer idleness. He also failed to do a stroke of work and bullied a very honest, and conscientious man, causing him to have a nervous breakdown.'

'I ought to have sent Eleanore round to him. She would have scared the living wits out of him!'

He had finished eating and sprung to his feet.

'All right. Dinner's over,' he said. The family got up and shuffled out.

For the first and only time during our friendship, I had a bite from Bob later on that evening. He, likewise, only received one bite from me, years later in July 1983 when I was suffering from Valium withdrawal and thought I was dying of a brain tumour. I will come to that later.

After the post-election dinner, Betty took me up to a beautifully decorated television room, known as the 'bird room' because of the large collection of porcelain birds in there. Betty showed me some family albums. Lying loose in one of them were some chest X-rays. I thought this was strange and I asked Betty whose they were and what they showed.

'They're Bob's X-rays. He had a lung removed.'

I knew about this already and couldn't think of anything appropriate to say.

'Did he now?' I said.

Betty went to bed and Bob came into the room saying there was an American thriller he wanted to watch. He asked me if I wanted to see it and I said I would. He sat on the sofa and I sat on the floor at his feet.

The film was totally incomprehensible. Even when my wits are at their best, I find American accents, particularly with voices speaking very fast, difficult, if not impossible to understand.

However, Bob appeared to understand the film and he found it extremely gripping. I started asking a lot of questions as is my habit during films. If I go to the cinema unaccompanied, I call for the usherette in the same way I would call for a taxi. I make her sit beside me to tell me what's going on. I tip 20p for every 'what did he say?' and 50p for every 'what is he doing?'

'Who's that man, Bob?'

Silence.

'Is he going to murder that woman?'

Silence.

'Is that the woman he's been taking out?'

Silence.

'Is that the woman's sister?'

Silence.

'I don't understand. Are they identical twins?'

It was at that point that I had my one and only bite.

'How the f***ing hell should I know!' he bellowed. 'You can see the film just as well as I can so shut up!'

'Yes, Bob.'

I made a mental note of the fact that Bob would not make a very co-operative cinema usherette.

The next day, I came down wearing a red miniskirt and patent high-heeled boots, covering part of the thigh. I had coffee. Then I went into Bob's study where I knew he would be working.

He seemed delighted to see me, either because of my apparel or my personality, probably both.

'Pamela rang earlier,' he said a little irritably. 'She wants you back. I don't want you to go. I'm going to miss you and I want you to come back here whenever you feel like it. You have a permanent invitation to my house, even if you only want to call in for one of your baths.' By the way, that fiery driver's waiting for you outside.'

'You're so kind,' I said. 'I really don't want to leave.'

'I'm not kind! There are a lot of untrustworthy people around who will only be interested in you because your father owns the *Telegraph*. I take you for what you are as a person and any time you have a problem, come straight to me. When you come back, we'll read *Pravda* together.'

We kissed each other goodbye. Then he said.

'Thank-you so much for all your hard work. We've helped each other. I've helped you become more self-assertive and aggressive and you've gone out of your way trying to help me retain my seat. You will write to me, won't you?'

'Yes, of course I will.'

I felt very sad. I said 'goodbye' to Betty and what children I could find. Then I went out to Mr Brightwell. Bob waved goodbye until the car was out of his eyeshot.

* * *

I returned to the Maxwells on my own invitation 3 months later. It was a Friday night and Bob had already gone to bed because he was exhausted.

Betty, some of the children and I were having breakfast in the kitchen overlooking the lawn. In came Bob, so obviously pleased to see me that it seemed as if he had been happily anticipating my visit for several days.

'Why didn't you tell me Eleanore was coming?' he said to Betty. 'If you'd told me before I would have been able to look forward to it.'

It's on remembering words like that that I become homicidal when I hear anyone criticizing Bob. The ordeal I had to bear was even worse after his death than in his lifetime, because the Press took advantage of the fact that the dead can't be libelled.

He took me for a walk round the garden and we spoke in Russian. The swimming pool was no longer in use. Its leaf-covered water was an uninviting shade of stagnant green.

Suddenly he picked me up as if I were a mere half stone and held me over the water, threatening to drop me. The incident showed me the prankish side of his nature which manifested itself whenever he wanted to become the child, Lajbi, again, the boy deprived of clothes, food, toys and jokes during his appallingly unhappy childhood.

He took me to his study while Jean was waiting for him. Jean and I greeted each other before Bob gave her instructions.

'How many people have died in the constituency, Miss Baddeley?'

'Only four, Mr Maxwell. I've sent the format letters to the appropriate next of kins with your signature on them.'

'Good. Any marriages for congratulations?'

'Yes, just one. The couple are ex-circus freak show performers. The man's working in a bank now.'

'His name?'

'Cyril Dibbs. He's a dwarf.'

Bob sat back in his heavy executive chair and lit a cigar.

'And his wife, is she also a dwarf?'

'Yes, Mr Maxwell.'

'Blimey! Some like it hot!' said Bob.

To this day, I have no idea what this remark meant, except that it sounded funny even if the humour couldn't be defined.

The family had acquired a singularly strange butler whose real name I can't remember. Bob addressed him as 'Genius' so I'll refer to him as that.

Genius came into my bedroom at 8.30 a.m. without knocking on the door. I had reformed my habit of getting up just before lunch and he found me naked. I was just about to go to the bathroom.

'Have you got any empty glasses in here?' asked Genius.

'No. I'm getting dressed for breakfast.'

'I'll leave the room, then,' he said after a long pause.

'Thank you. I think that would be the best thing to do in the circumstances.'

I often stayed with the family on the weekend nearest to my birthday. I sat on Bob's right. He was in a good mood that day and we were laughing and joking, but during the meal a family row broke out. Ghislaine was allowed home from her boarding- school each weekend and on Sunday she wanted to spend the whole day riding. Bob complained that Sunday was the only day of the week he could see her and if she spent that day riding, he wouldn't be able to spend the amount of time in her company that he wished to.

Ghislaine rebelled against him and told him that it was unfair of him to make such demands on her. Isabel, the sensible, law-abiding, somewhat bossy older sister, took her father's side and argued with Ghislaine.

'You must be fair to him and stop being so selfish,' she said. 'He hardly sees anything of you.'

'Mind your own business. Sunday's the only day of the week I get to go riding.'

I was becoming extremely bored with this trivial argument so I decided to take part in it.

'If you spend your time worrying about what you can't do,' I said to Ghislaine, 'You will never benefit from what you can do.'

'You're absolutely right,' said Bob. 'Besides, this is not an interesting conversation.' He turned to me. 'So it's your birthday today? What year were you born?'

I automatically took 3 years off my age.

'All right. I'm going down to the cellar to find a bottle of wine for that year and I bet you won't be able to drink all of it in one go.'

'I bet I will.'

He left the room and came back 5 minutes later with a full-sized, dusty bottle of red wine for what he took to be the year of my birth. He opened it and for some reason put it on his left out of my reach. I leant across him, excitedly but discourteously in an effort to grab the bottle.

'Don't be so impatient, Missy!' He gave me a smack on the back of the hand. 'You can't have the wine till you've finished your champagne.'

I was feeling in a naughty mood. I gulped down the champagne and reached out for the wine. Bob put his hand on mine but I struggled to move my hand which was a silly thing to do because it was in a vice like grip. For a big man, Bob had tiny hands with a Rottweiler's grip.

'But you promised I could have the bottle of wine after I'd finished the champagne.'

'All right, all right, Basso Profundo. You're the greediest pussycat I've ever met. Here's your wine. I bet you can't drink the lot.'

'Papa, is all this wise?' Betty leant anxiously across the table.

'Yes! The girl's as tough as an ox. There's nothing she can't do. You watch her.'

Encouraged by these words, I let Bob fill my glass to the brim and threw it down my throat. I handed him the empty glass and the ritual was repeated and continued until the contents of the bottle had been consumed.

I didn't feel sick but I lost all my inhibitions.

'My God, you drank it!' said Bob.

'Yes, you never thought I would, did you?'

Everyone at the table went silent. Ian on the right, a cheerful, vivacious, friendly boy and a witty conversationalist, looked at me and then appeared worried. Perhaps he thought I was going to be sick.

'Bob, I want to tell you an absolutely hilarious joke,' I said.

'Get on with it then.'

'All right. There was this Irishman who went to an employment agency.'

' "Where did you work?" asked the agency.

' "In a mortuary," replied the Irishman.

' "Why did you leave?" asked the agency.

' "I was fired," said the Irishman.

' "Why were you fired?"

' "For bunging the corpses doon onto the slab instead of layin' 'em gently, and after layin' 'em doon for fockin' 'em from behoind." '

There was an ominous silence. I looked at Ian who seemed perturbed. Then I looked at Bob and his appearance shocked me beyond description. Mercifully, Betty did not understand the thick Irish accent I mimicked. Neither did Ghislaine. Bob actually turned pale green and began to sweat. There was a mild tremor in his hands. I feared I had made him ill but was so intoxicated I couldn't remember what I'd said. He rose partially from his chair and with his left hand, reached out for a bell which he rang.

A Filipino lady, recognizing the sound of the bell to be the master's ring, scurried into the room.

'You rang, Mr Maxwell?'

Bob eased himself to his feet with what seemed like exaggerated difficulty and clutched the table as if about to have a heart attack.

'Mr Maxwell, are you all right?'

When he spoke, he sounded as if he had to drag out his words. He walked from the room with a staggering, lurching gait, supporting himself on the backs of chairs.

'Mr Maxwell, do you need help?'

'I'm going to my room,' he said in a slow deliberate voice, an octave even lower than his normal tone. 'Would you please bring me a tray of hot sweet tea.'

'Ian!' I said.

'Yes.'

'Your father, has he been taken ill? Have I damaged him in some way?' I demanded hysterically.

'There's one thing I must tell you and that is this,' he began. 'Dad's about the strongest man on earth but whatever you do, don't ever talk to him about necrophiliacs or necrophilia.'

'Why?' I asked, stupidly.

'Because it cracks him like a nut. It may be something to do with his experiences in the war. He just can't take it.'

'My God, I had no idea. Anyway it was partly his fault. He made me drink that wine. I didn't mean to harm him. Should I go up to his room and say I'm sorry?'

Ian banged his forehead with the palm of his outstretched hand.

'No. For God's sake don't do that. Just let him sleep it off. He might even have forgotten it by the time he comes down.'

'What's going on?' asked Betty in a baffled tone. What's wrong with Papa, Ian?'

'Nothing. He just felt a bit under the weather. Don't worry, he's fine.'

'Do you really think he will forget about it by the time he's finished his rest?' I asked.

'Yes, I should think so. The man's got a hell of a lot of other things on his mind, besides Irishmen screwing the dead!'

Kevin, who did not take the episode as seriously as Ian and who was sitting at the other end of the table, might not have witnessed the full incident but he must have known that there had been some trouble regarding a bottle of wine. He also knew that I was doing a thesis on the Marquis de Sade.

Later that afternoon, Bob came down and interviewed a blonde secretary in his study. Kevin entered the room with a glass in his hand, mistaking the blonde woman, who had her back to him, for me.

'Have another glass of wine,' he said exuberantly. 'Vintage Château de Sade!'

'F*** off, Kevin!' said Bob.

'I liked the sexy blonde secretary you interviewed, Dad,' said Ian at dinner. 'She seemed much better than the one with the terrible acne and the awful legs.'

Bob turned on his son.

'I don't want to hear that kind of talk, Ian because it's cruel.'

'Sorry, Dad.'

I admit that I did not distinguish myself at Headington Hill Hall that weekend. On Sunday morning, I got up very late and found Bob walking across the hall.

'Hullo. I hear you got up very early this morning,' he said. Another weekend, when I thought I could get away with repeating the same misdemeanour, his reaction was tougher.

It was about 12.45. I came into the living room where Bob and the family were having pre-lunch drinks. He always served the drinks from behind the bar, like a publican. He seemed happy when doing this and did it with a beaming smile.

'May I have a gin and tonic, please, Bob?'

He came out from behind the bar and walked with me to the other end of the room away from everyone else.

'Look, you must get up in the mornings,' he said, his voice raised in anger. 'Do you realize the maid was unable to come in and make the bed?'

There was something inexplicably comical about his last sentence. I imagined a timid, cowering woman, carrying dusters, mops and cloths in a bucket, waiting outside, afraid to knock on the door.

I smiled, took his hand in mine and kissed it and rolled my eyes at him. He softened.

'Naughty pussycat,' he said, 'come over and have your gin and tonic.'

Just before leaving for London that evening. I had coffee with Bob in the Pergamon offices next to his house.

'What books are you studying at University?' he asked.

I told him I was doing *A la reserche du temps perdu* (Proust) and I confessed I was reading it in English because reading French gave me migraines.

He laughed and said that it was idleness and not migraines which deterred me from reading it in French. I told him I found Proust repetitive, tedious and superficial, adding that I was utterly fed up with his greater preoccupation with objects and smells than sympathetic or deep rooted-sentiment. I also told him that far too much coverage was given to a biscuit and the grossly overrated significance attached to the biscuit in Marcel's eyes.

'Why the hell didn't Proust call this bloody, exasperating work "Biscuits I have known"? I said.

Bob got irritated. He obviously thought my attitude was insensitive.

'The biscuit may not have seemed important to you,' he said sternly, 'but you should understand that it was very important indeed to the boy.'

Our conversation was interrupted. Jean Baddeley entered the room to remind Bob that he had to go out on business. He was dressed in a red and white pin-striped suit. Apart from his terrifying father, Jean was the only person who could control Bob.

'Mr Maxwell, I'm not going anywhere with you until you change into a more appropriate suit. The one you are wearing is extremely vulgar.'

'All right, all right, Miss Baddeley. I'm always being ordered about by hens.'

When I returned to London, I sent twenty red roses to Betty with a note attached, saying I was sorry about any misunderstanding regarding the bottle of wine. My unfortunate conduct was forgiven and forgotten.

The Maxwells invited me again for the weekend 3 weeks hence. I was walking in the garden on Saturday morning and saw Ghislaine running towards me.

'Can you do me a great favour and drive me to the stables?'

'I don't see why not. Where are they?'

'In the country, 10 miles away from here. Is your car the silver one?'

'Yes.' We went to the car. 'We'll have to get a move on. Otherwise, we'll be late for lunch,' I said.

'This is a nice car.'

'Yes, it's not bad. Jump in.'

Once she was in the passenger's seat and I had moved up the drive, she turned to me abruptly.

'By the way, Daddy said you're not to play Beethoven's Ninth when you're driving because he says you have a lot of accidents, drive far too fast and crash into the backs of other cars when you listen to it. Otherwise, he said you're a not too bad a driver.'

I thought she was rather impertinent and suddenly wondered whether she had asked her parents if I could drive her.

'Does you father know I'm taking you to the stables?'

'No. I never asked him.'

I did an emergency stop.

'Do you mean you asked me to take you off the premises without his permission?'

'Yes. I don't always ask his permission when I want to do things.'

'Is that because you think he might say "no"?'

'I suppose you could say that.'

I was furious with her for inviting me to get into an invidious position.

'Look, Ghislaine, it's extremely naughty and irresponsible of you to trick me into taking you off the premises. You are your father's property and if you were to come to harm, I would be answerable for it.'

I reversed down the ramp-infested, sinuous drive and came to a halt.

'Get out of the car, Ghislaine, and go into the house and ask your father's permission.'

She got out. She looked pretty and sultry with her long brown pony-tail, her large, almond-shaped eyes and face that had formed itself into a pronounced pout.

'It's OK. I don't want to go now,' she said.

'You've been so kind to me, Bob,' I said at the end of the weekend.

'I'm not kind!' His tone was almost angry. I was always telling him how kind he was and he invariably gave me the same backhandedly touching answer.

He often saw my father at press meetings in London.

'How's that smashing daughter of yours Michael?' he said on one of these occasions, and once when he saw Nicky in London he told him he was my surrogate father.

I never failed to look forward to my weekends at Headington Hill Hall.

Genius, who found it extremely difficult to tell the difference between wine and port, poured port into the high-stemmed, intricately decorated Venetian glasses.

Bob got very irritated.

'Oh, no, no, no, no, Genius!' he shouted. 'This is port. We want wine!'

Genius went out and produced a bottle of wine and a tray of clean glasses during the cheese course. The unfortunate man bungled again.

Bob had ordered more glasses so that the cheaper wine consumed at lunch could be supplemented by a more costly wine, a crate of which had been delivered to the house by a friend of the family.

Genius poured the costly wine into glasses still containing the ordinary wine. Bob was furious.

'No, no, no, no,no, Genius!' he repeated, this time more angrily than the first.

'I'm sorry, Mr Maxwell, I don't understand your instructions.'

'Just take away all the glasses and start again!'

Bob suffered from unnerving mood swings, ranging from playful euphoria through being surrounded by those he loved, and life for the sake of life, to what seemed like impenetrable gloom.

I surmised this to be comprised of a number of complex factors. Until the day he died, he had memories of his family being herded on to trains bound for the gas chambers.

His greatest childhood love was for his mother, Hannah Hoch. I saw a picture of her once. She closely resembled Isabel's twin sister, Christine, except that she was much stouter. In the picture, she wore a simple, dark-coloured dress with a large collar and an array of buttons on the front of her dress.

Her face had a look of *Mona Lisa* serenity. Bob, known to her as Lajbi, was her favourite child and I could imagine him running behind her everywhere she went, clinging to her skirts.

'I love hiding behind ladies' petticoats,' he once said to me at lunch when he was in a relaxed mood.

I hated it when he was depressed, fearing old age and loneliness, fearing the loss of his daughters when they would eventually marry, fearing recessions and bankruptcy and the possible demise of his loved ones. I'm sure he often looked back to the death of his oldest son, Michael, whom he wanted to succeed him and who lay in a coma for several years before he died.

Most of all, his horrendous memories of the Holocaust haunted him all his life and even the presence of his wife and children was sometimes equally as incapable of lifting the black cloud from his head as a bamboo fence shielding territory from enemy cannon.

When in these moods he seldom spoke and did not welcome any conversational overtures. Sometimes he would unconsciously interrogate a family member within earshot and ask one of his arresting questions, of which, for some unknown reason, Ghislaine, his favourite was often the recipient.

He seldom did this to me when he was in one of these moods but he did question me one day when I was sitting next to him. I can tell when someone near me is depressed, whether they show it or not. That day

Bob definitely was, even though he had recently won £50,000 from a lawsuit against *Private Eye*. I decided not to speak until he spoke to me because there is something formidable and hard to handle about a depressed person.

Lunch was almost silent. I felt very sad to see that Bob looked so tired and had put on weight, although his facial beauty was still intact. He turned to me very suddenly, speaking quite quietly.

'Tell me, Eleanore, when you're not looking ravishingly beautiful, how do you occupy your time?'

The compliment was like an elixir. I thanked him but he only wanted a concise answer.

'I work for a series of agencies who send me to London hospitals where I follow the surgeons on ward rounds. I write down everything they say about the patients they see, log it into a computer and enter it into their files. Sometimes, I am sent to the post mortem room to take notes during autopsies.

'No gory talk please,' said Bob.

'Papa, she's been doing that for years and years,' said Betty to him from across the table.'Do you know what she said? She said she had been out of work for two whole days. I had to laugh.'

'I don't see why', said Bob. 'Two days is two days' lost. How much are they paying you?'

The rate was £6 an hour.

'I get £13.50 an hour,' I said. 'I wouldn't settle for less than that.'

'Good! You could take us all out to dinner at the Ritz with that,' said Bob.

I was feeling a bit better because his depression seemed to be shifting.

'Bob, will you give me a signed copy of your book about the *Private Eye* case — *Malice in Wonderland?*'

Bob picked up a leg of chicken with his fingers and shoved it into his mouth.

'I don't see why not. You gave me a signed copy of *Never Alone with Rex Malone*. Do you remember?'

'I don't forget the titles of my books easily,' I said.

He laughed.

'Of course I'll sign it for you — as one author to another.'

He got up abruptly from the table and went over to Philip.

'Come on, Philip,' he said, 'there's work to do,' and disappeared through the door dividing the dining room from the living room. Compulsively, I got up and followed the father and son. I had a burning

71

urge to talk to Bob even if I had no idea what I wanted to talk to him about.

Bob tried to close the door but because I had taken a large quantity of Speed, my demeanour was manic and irrational.

He was closing the door gently but I threw my weight against it.

'Bob, I'm not leaving here until you give me a signed copy of your book and I've said goodbye to you.'

'Goodbye!' he said. He and Philip were sitting down earnestly talking shop. I was irritated. I wasn't prepared to leave until he had given me what I wanted. I opened the door and went straight in. I think he was secretly impressed by my persistent, Speed-induced approach as his face softened into a large smile.

'Come to the study for a moment,' he said, his tone friendly. 'Of course, you shall have the book you said you wanted.'

He led me in by the hand, just as an adult holds on to a child to stop it crossing a road. He took the book from the top of a pile and wrote a friendly, but not particularly interesting message in it, followed by his signature.

'There you are, Missy?'

I thanked him and held the book to my chest.

'Turn round. Let's have a look at you.'

I did as he asked. I was wearing a yellow leather suit with a pair of red snake skin stiletto boots for which he had expressed a liking on other occasions. He also liked my collection of leather suits so I wore one of them every time I saw him, except during heatwaves.

'You look really smashing!' he said.

Yet another elixir. I rolled my eyes at him and put my arms round his neck while he kissed me on the mouth. (Not lingeringly).

'You're a lovely man, Bob,' I said.

My visits to the house were frequent. This time, I only went down there for lunch one stifling hot Saturday in July. I was going through a phase of Valium addiction and my doctor at that time, whom I got on very badly with, refused to get me off the drug gradually. Instead, he stopped prescribing it altogether.

Physically, I felt iller than I had ever felt in my life. A gong seemed to be booming inside my head. I felt dizzy and terrifyingly faint. I was sweating so much that my clothes were clinging to me like limpets. Accompanied by these symptoms were acute anxiety and shakes.

I didn't realize the addictive properties of Valium. I had been taking 50 — 100 mg a night for insomnia and was forced to stop abruptly. At the time, I had no idea that the drug was addictive and that I was going through Valium withdrawal and I assumed I had a brain tumour. I felt that I was on the way out and I had a yearning to see the Maxwells first.

When I got to the gates of the house, guarded by an over-vigilant watchman, he found my voice so strange that he had to phone through to Bob to see if I could enter.

Once I arrived at the house, I had a drink, first with Ian who had to rush off to represent his father at a funeral, and then I had another drink with Betty.

I wondered whether to tell Ian that I felt ill but decided not to. I thought the alcohol would drain my symptoms.

'Have another,' said Ian.

'I'd better not. I'll only go under.'

'Don't worry. You won't go under. I can guarantee that.'

Betty came in just as Ian was leaving. I couldn't see her in focus and struggled to disguise my condition. She talked at length about numerous subjects including the activities of her children, skiing resorts, her visits to Val d'Isère and Bob's dissatisfaction with Ghislaine's wild lifestyle. Ghislaine was now in her early 20s and Bob and she had been having a lot of arguments about her morals.

'Where's Bob now?' I asked.

'He's in the Pergamon offices, working on something with Jean. He should be here by now. Why don't we walk up there to see if we can get them to come down?'

We left the house and went towards the offices. I could hardly put one foot in front of the other. I held Betty's arm.

Once in the Pergamon offices I sat down and bent over with my head between my knees. I told Betty I was feeling faint because of the heat. I took that precaution so that if I fainted in front of Bob, she would provide an adequate explanation.

Within 15 minutes, Bob came down into the hall with Jean. He had no idea I was coming and appeared overjoyed to see me, like a big puppy. He told me I looked prettier than ever and I held his arm tightly while walking down the steps. I was terrified I was going to faint.

I gave him a gift-wrapped package containing caviare.

'May I open my present now?'

'Yes, of course, I said. I've brought you some of your favourite Beluga.'

He was as delighted as a small boy.

'Betty, go and put this in the fridge,' he said a bit bossily.

He started talking to me in Russian but the words came only as sounds and made no sense. I do recall, though, that he said he was going to Moscow to visit President Andropov to which I stupidly replied 'Why?'

He continued to speak Russian, smiling at me all the time as we approached the house. The Rolls with his personal number-plate was parked between the pillars at the entrance.

I didn't know whether I was speaking Russian, German, French or English. Finally, I pointed to the Rolls and said what a beautiful Mercedes he had. (In German which I thought was Russian.)

'Let's go indoors,' he said. 'You're ill, aren't you?'

'No, I'm not.'

'Yes, you are.' 'I'm very worried about the kind of company you keep in London.'

'The company I keep? I only keep decent company. What do you mean?'

Bob took three pre-lunch sticks of celery from one of the occasional tables, dipped them into a saucer containing a creamy-looking sauce and shoved them into his mouth.

'Are you mixing with Sloane Rangers? I have reason to suspect you are.'

'Well I'm not,' I said, my voice raised in an effort to hide my symptoms. 'I hate Sloane Rangers.'

'I'm interviewing a man this afternoon,' said Bob, 'a man who is an authority on Sloane Rangers. Would you like to meet him?'

'Oh, for Christ's sake, Bob! Do I have to?' I shouted.

The tension was immediately broken. There were times when Bob appeared to like women shouting at him and he roared with laughter.

'Hey, I liked that,' he said. 'You need to eat and we're having lunch now. Go out there and sit down.'

By this time I felt so ill that I genuinely thought I was going to drop dead. I have always believed it to be the height of bad manners to die, either in someone's house or their garden, and I hoped that if the Reaper wanted to take me, he would be reasonable enough to do so once I had got back to London.

Bob, Jean and Betty came and took their seats at the table.

It was overbearingly hot eating in the garden. Bob wolf-whistled for Oping, the cook and I laughed out loud.

'What are you laughing at?' he asked, smiling.

'I like the way you whistle. My sister whistles like that but I still don't know how to do it.'

74

I knew that if the conversation continued in English, I'd probably be able to hold out. There was comic relief when the family dog, Angara, named after either a Czechoslovakian town or a river, forced its way under the glass table and licked Oping's legs when she was serving.

Bob pulled back his chair.

'Do you think we could get the dog out?' he said.

Jean talked at length about sheets and pillowcases and linen and laundry. I was relieved not to have to speak because even my tongue was aching and my mouth and throat felt like sand.

'All right, all right, Jean,' said Bob, 'poor Eleanore doesn't want to sit here while you talk about sheets and I haven't seen her for ages. Come on, Eleanore, let's have some comic relief. Tell me about your outrageous adventures.'

I'd given up working as a translator and was then engaged in full-time freelance work for doctors and surgeons which fuelled my interest in the macabre and gave me book fodder.

Translating work, though challenging to the brain, was becoming soul-destroying. The people I was sent to showed little respect either for me or my intelligence. Often, when I asked for sugar in my coffee, they told me I'd have to bring my own, combined with coffee and milk. I told them I was too important to rattle across London with pots and pans like some destitute tinker. Secretaries, who only spoke English, seemed to resent me because I spoke French and Russian. At one establishment, a secretary treated me like a peasant and told me to monitor her personal calls.

'Find out who it is?' she kept asking me in an artificial upper class-accent.

'Come and find out your bloody self!' I shouted. 'I'm not your lackey.'

Bob was sitting there laughing and the audience he was giving me cheered me although I still felt very ill. I lowered my head and said under my breath, 'Reaper, Reaper, go away. Save it for another day.'

I then said that the secretary had started to put apple cores and orange peel on to my computer keys. I lost my temper with her and punched her in the jaw and was fired.

'Christ turned the other cheek so why couldn't you?' said Bob, expressing an attitude I felt to be totally out of character.

'Christ died young,' I said. Bob looked shocked for some reason and tilted his head back and pursed his lips as he always did when he was shocked or displeased. I gave him a beaming smile to disarm him.

'Your stories are killing me, he said. 'Come on, tell me some more.'

'Last week, I was sent to work for a team of psychiatrists in a geriatric hospital. I went to Personnel where a woman told me she had had to double-book me and she didn't even say "sorry". It meant I wouldn't be able to find work for the rest of the week.'

'In that case, you should have hit her on the head with a shoe,' said Bob.

I continued the narrative.

' "Would you say something like that to a taxi driver?" I said, pinning her against the wall.

' "No," she whispered.

' "Want to know why?" I asked.

' "Why?" she eventually managed to splutter.

' "Because a taxi driver would slit your throat. So would I if I had a knife." '

Oping came to the table to tell Bob a call had come through from Moscow but he wanted to finish the conversation first.

'All right, so the next day I take it you went back with your knife.'

'With your knife, with your knife, with your knife.'

These words were going round and round in my head like a bee. I found myself in the house. Betty and Jean must have helped me away from the table after Bob had gone out to take his call.

'You've been very kind,' I said to Betty, 'but I must go back to London now.'

'You're not fit to drive. You'll have an accident.'

Like a whale, I had a passionate yearning to die in the city in which I was born and raised and lived in all my life. My symptoms were still just as bad and if anything worse.

'I do feel ever so much better now,' I lied. 'Besides, I have a sick relative I promised to have tea with and she hasn't got a telephone.'

'All right,' said Betty, 'as long as you feel fit enough to drive.' I kissed her goodbye and saw Bob in the hall. I had completely lost my wits as well as feeling ill. My vision was so impaired I could hardly recognize him and I identified him with a benevolent doctor figure and asked him to give me a typhoid injection.

He didn't answer but walked me out to the car. I drove back to London in the slow lane all the way with all four windows open.

I booked myself into the London clinic and sent for a solicitor to make out a Will. I remained there for 6 weeks and was in bed all day, except on an occasion when I had to have a brain scan and had to be pushed down the street in a wheelchair. My head was so heavy I couldn't hold it up and my hair was tangled and unbrushed.

After 6 weeks, I suddenly had no symptoms. I no longer felt ill in any way. The Valium withdrawal was complete. My friends and relatives who visited me remarked irritatingly that I was something of a hypochondriac.

* * *

I completed the manuscript of *Never Alone With Rex Malone* in the summer of 1985. The book started in 2054 and looked back to the late twentieth Century when Bob and Betty, known as Rex Malone and Hortense Malone respectively were the most revered couple in Britain. Natalie Klein, modelled on myself, fought ruthlessly and unscrupulously for them in any way she could.

I knew I couldn't send it to the publisher until Bob had found out about it. I was terrified he would refuse to let me publish it because of the extreme ribaldry which peppered its pages. I grew more and more worried and had to walk out of the film *Passage to India* which my friends had taken me to. I was unbearably hot, and acutely anxious.

The next morning at 7.30, I started to get *Rex Malone* moving. I rang Ian in his flat at the Barbican.

'Ian, I've got something very important to tell you,' I said in a voice which might have indicated that my whole family had been run over by a tram.

'Well tell me, then. Why all this hassle?'

'I've just written a book in which your father is the main character. I've made him out to be a national hero.'

Ian was taken aback and didn't speak straight away.

'Hullo, Ian, are you there?'

'Yes. This man in your book — is he recognizable as Bob?' (I was interested that he did not say 'my father.')

'Good God, yes! Your father must see it, though, before I send it off.'

'I don't know why you're so worried. I'm going to stay with my father this weekend. Why don't you send the manuscript round to me in a taxi and I'll take it to him and he can see it? What are you calling him?'

'Rex Malone.'

'Jesus!'

I sent the manuscript to Ian, having rubbed some of its pages with heather given to me by a gypsy. (I'm incurably superstitious.) It was as easy as that. Ian said he'd ring me after the weekend. I was so nervous that Bob would think it too coarse and macabre that I spent Saturday and Sunday in bed.

Ian's call came early on Monday morning.'

'Is it all right?' I asked hysterically.

'Of course, its all right,' he said. 'I gave the book to Dad to read and also read aloud to him the passages I thought he'd missed.'

'What did he say?'

'He was extraordinarily flattered and amused. He had a good laugh. He wants you to come down next Saturday.'

'When on Saturday and until when?'

'Twelve noon. We're having some of Anne's friends for drinks. You can stay for dinner if you want.'

'On Saturday, I put on a turquoise shirt and matching turquoise trousers tucked into the red snake skin stiletto heeled boots.

I drove, reaching speeds of 110 miles per hour down the M40 in a state of euphoria. As I came closer to Oxford, I began to feel exhausted and sick in anticipation of Bob's words about *Rex Malone*. I pulled in and took what I thought were five Speed pills to bring me to my original state of euphoria which my nervousness had killed.

Instead I took five Maxalon as the two bottles and the pills looked similar. Maxalon, taken in such a quantity, induces terrifying gloom which can last for two weeks. It hit me 20 minutes after I'd swallowed it and I couldn't understand what was wrong.

I got there having called at a pub for mood-elevating liquor which wasn't nearly strong enough to get me back to normal.

Oping opened the door for me at Headington Hill Hall.

'Hullo, I said, 'How are you keeping?'

'Very well, very well, thank-you, Eleanore. Mr Maxwell is waiting for you. He wants to see you.'

'Where is he?'

'On the lawn.'

I started to get very hot and agitated. I panicked and went upstairs and took a bath.

I found Bob at a table outside accompanied by Jean, Ghislaine and some strange-looking, heavily-sweating man in black, talking about prayer books. Ghislaine and Bob were quarrelling because he said her dress was indecent and she was threatening to pour a bowl of strawberries over his head.

'You can't do that, Ghislaine,' I said across the table. If I did that to my father, he'd ask me to leave the house.'

Bob's attention was distracted.

'There you are!' he said to me. 'Oping told me you'd arrived half an hour ago. What have you been doing before you came outside?'

'My hands were covered in oil. I had to go upstairs and scrub it off.'

'He raised his head and pursed his lips which he always did when he knew he was being lied to.

'Well, whatever you did, you look smashing and it's nice to see you again. By the way, I know all about your book. I've read it.'

'Indeed? May I ask if you enjoyed it?'

'Yes, it was one long laugh. I didn't know what had hit me. I liked the way you wrote about me. I was absolutely flabbergasted!'

Ghislaine interrupted which annoyed me because I thought Bob was going to say more.

'Do you know something, Eleanor? My father is being an absolute pain.'

'I'm afraid that's none of my business,' I said.

Bob and Ghislaine started wrestling. I became very bored. I was furious with myself for taking the wrong pills. I turned to Jean and made amicable conversation with her.

Bob left the table to have his rest. It seemed as if the sun had gone in.

I waited all afternoon for him to come back and, to pass the time, I talked to the guests and went swimming.

He returned at six, wearing a white, bath-towel dressing gown and sat down. I kissed Betty goodbye and then knelt at Bob's feet and let him take my hand in his and waited for him to kiss me goodbye.

'Goodbye, Missy, and good luck with your book.'

* * *

Considering Bob was not the easiest of men to work for, Genius stayed on a few years until the tragedy that made him redundant.

I visited the house again. Bob landed by helicopter a few feet away from the lunch table in the garden. His timing was immaculate. He arrived just as the food was being put on the table.

He greeted me in his usual affectionate, friendly way but seemed irritated that I had my fingers in my ears to protect them from the whirring rotary blades.

Apart from Bob, Betty and Jean and a strange looking young man who never spoke, even to say 'good-morning,' had taken their places at the table.

I had noted over the years that Bob saved all his charms and flirtatious chivalry for female company which is why women found him irresistible. However, this pattern of social conduct was rarely directed towards members of his own sex which is why men very frequently disliked him and why many women loved him.

The pilot turned the rotary blades off. Bob remained standing while the stranger remained glued to his chair, looking at the plate of fresh salmon which had been placed in front of him.

I sensed Bob was in another depression and that his mood was poor. He directed his piercing black eyes at the younger man.

'Who are you?' he demanded. His tone was hostile.

The man didn't answer. Nor did he rise to his feet when his host addressed him. The question was repeated at a shout and the man still failed to answer. I got the giggles.

'Who's he?' said Bob to me.

'Your guess is as good as mine. He's been sitting in silence all morning and I couldn't get his name out of him, for love nor money either. Maybe he's an escaped Trappist monk.'

I turned to the man.

'You really must say who you are and rise to your feet when your host addresses you. For Christ's sake tell him your name!'

Finally, the stranger answered although I can't remember the name he gave.

'Why are you here?' asked Bob, still standing while his guest remained seated.

'I'm here because you asked me to come here,' said the man.

'I don't remember asking you. How do you earn your keep?'

'I'm on the Mirror,' said the man while I struggled to keep a straight face. 'It was you who interviewed me last week.'

Bob sat down between Jean and Betty. For some incomprehensible reason, he addressed the stranger in French which he spoke with a thick East European accent.

'What have you learned since joining the Mirror?' asked Bob impatiently, strangely addressing him as 'tu.'

The man bumbled on and on in a monotonous, sleep inducing voice. I dreaded to think what his prose would be like, if he were called upon to write.

Bob sometimes tended to get a bit rough when he was depressed, although, with a few exceptions, women were pretty immune to the sharper side of his tongue.

'I want to ask you a question, Bob,' I said, calling across the table.

'All right. What's your question?'

'A film producer says he's interested in making a film of *Never Alone With Rex Malone*. I said I'd have to ask your permission first. Do you give me your permission or not?'

'I give you my entire permission. Any idea who's going to play me?'

'I'd like to get Ben Gazzara to do it. He's American but Peter O'Toole could dub the voice because his voice is not at all unlike yours. B.G.'s very good. Do you approve of him?'

Bob finished his huge mouthful of salmon, peas and boiled potatoes and took a slug of Chablis to wash them down.

'No,' he said.

'Why?' He's very attractive, you know.'

'No, he's not!'

'No normal man finds another man attractive. Women go mad when they see him.'

'I don't care whether they go mad or not. What's wrong with Robert Mitchum?'

'Nothing, but I may not have the last decision. There's another question I need to ask. There's a possibility that *Never Alone With Rex Malone* will be reprinted. May I please quote you as saying you were absolutely flabbergasted by it when I saw you in July 1985?'

'Yes.'

'May I also quote you as having said you just didn't know what had hit you which you said the last time we met?'

'No.'

The silent young man entered the conversation at this point. I was amazed that he was capable of speaking,

'Mr Maxwell, I'm told the Head of the Ethiopian Government presented you with a gold cup engraved with an acknowlededgment of your kindness and generosity towards the famine victims.'

I considered the man an awful suck-up and knew he would speak ill of Bob after leaving his house on account of the latter's extreme abruptness. However, it is indisputable that Bob's initial approach to the man was singularly unfriendly.

Bob put two fingers in each side of his mouth and gave one of his wolf-whistles. Genius hurried to the table with his hands clasped in front of him.

'What can I do for you, Mr Maxwell?'

'There's a gold cup with an engraving on it on the shelf in the library area next door to the living room. Bring it to the table.'

Genius scuttled off. He spent a long time looking for the cup which indicated it was somewhere else.

He approached the table, his head lowered as if mounting the steps of a scaffold.

'It's not where you said it was, Mr Maxwell.'

Bob looked exasperated. He rose from his chair and walked towards the house with Genius following him sheepishly like a lap-dog.

The cup was not indeed where Bob had said it was. It was in one of the offices adjacent to the hall. He brought it back to the table with Genius still following him.

'It wasn't your fault, Genius,' he said, 'so you can dry your tears.'

The cup was shown to the tongueless guest who managed only to make obsequious comments about the engraving.

Bob saw through him, his artifice and no doubt his fear. It was clear he despised him.

'I understand Ghislaine's got a business going, selling executive gifts,' I said.

'You understand right,' said Bob, who was a singularly poor conversationlist that day.

When he had finished eating, he wolf-whistled again for Genius.

'Have you ever read a story by M.R. James called *Oh Whistle to me and I'll come to you, my lad*?' I asked.

'No,' said Bob.

By this time, Genius had arrived at the table.

'Will you get the pilot out of the house and bring him here.'

'Yes, Mr Maxwell.'

Genius hurried to the house where he found the pilot who came to the table immediately.

'I'm leaving now,' said Bob.

I got up and kissed him goodbye and he uttered an extraordinary Freudian slip.

'Good luck with your buck!' he said and was helped into the helicopter by the pilot. The ear-splitting rotary blades started whirring and the next minute it was in the sky.

Good God! thought I. The man's even more eccentric than I am!

In June 1988, Bob celebrated his 65th birthday. He had three lavish parties, one on 10 June which was the actual date of his birthday, another on 11 June and yet another on 12 June. I certainly found this extremely strange.

The one on 11 June appeared to me to be the most pleasant since it took place in the middle of the day. I had not received an invitation so I just turned up. I knew Bob used to do that and I was sure he'd be pleased to see me.

It was a very cold day for the time of year so I wore white, tight-fitting, leather trousers, a white V-necked sweater and Bob's favourite red snake skin, stiletto-heeled boots over the trousers I wore, matching red ear-rings and jewellery. My hair had just been done and I had also had a facial. I looked terrific.

The guard, to whom I was known by name and sight, stopped me at the gate. I leant out of the car.

'Hullo there. Long time no see. I'm Eleanor Berry and I've lost my invitation card, blast it. How are you keeping?'

The guard let me in.

The lawns were covered with a marquee. I went inside and saw a buffet and a myriad of tables at which people, whose faces I didn't recognize, guzzled. A cinema screen showed a film about Bob and his achievements. I got very excited and started to drink. Later, I found Jean. A *Mirror* photographer took pictures of her and me standing together.

'Have you seen Bob recently.' I asked.

'Not recently. He's been moving all over the place.'

I went round asking the eaters questions. The alcohol had made me very manic.

'He came through here 10 minutes ago,' said a woman turning towards me.

'Then where did he go?' I said clutching her arm and the expression on her face showed she thought I was mad.

'Where is he? Where is he? You've got to take me to him — now!'

'I can't. I've never met him.'

'You mean you don't know him? Why are you here then?'

'My name was taken from the telephone directory, I suppose.'

'What the hell are you talking about? Do you think I'm going to believe that?'

I moved on to another table and harassed its occupants in a similar manner; then I saw one of the Maxwell twins, leading a tiny child by the hand, walking through.

'Christine!' I shouted.

'No. It's Isabel.'

'Sorry about that.' I peered piercingly into her eyes.' Isabel, you *must* take me to your father. Where is he?'

'He's in the house. By the way I liked your *Rex Malone* even though it was a bit macabre.'

'Never mind the book! Please come with me to your father.'

'All right, calm down. Whatever's the matter?'

'Nothing. I just want to be taken to your father.'

'I'm going to see him myself. We'll go together.'

I couldn't keep up with Isabel because my stiletto heels kept sticking in the grass. She waited for me. Then she took me to her father. Her small son, Alexander, had painted the cover of a picture book. It was a gift for Bob.

Bob was standing in an inner chamber. I didn't know which room it was because its ceiling and walls were draped with white cloth like an Arab's tent.

'Hullo, Bob. Happy birthday,' I said and kissed him.

As always, he was pleased to see me. He introduced me to men of his age.

'This beautiful woman's name is Eleanor Berry and I'm one of her greatest admirers. When she was very young, she joined the Communist Party and went to Russia alone, having taught herself to speak Russian like a bloody native. She's got guts.'

He was unusually talkative that day because he was happy. He added:- 'She's got a hell of a lot of stories to tell you about her adventures. Once, she worked in a mortuary. After that she got a job as a temporary nanny and lasted for 10 minutes.'

There was general laughter. Then Bob turned to the 3-year-old boy who gave him the picture book. The cover was worded in a childlike hand probably helped by an adult. 'To Granddad who lives in a helicopter all day.'

Bob laughed and picked the small boy up. A black cloud went over my head because I had lost his attention.

Isabel helped herself to crudités and turned to me.

'Why did your nanny job only last for 10 minutes?'

'I don't know, I went to the house and found the children's mother in the kitchen. I introduced myself. 'Would you bring your children into the kitchen, please,' I said.

'She called them, giving me a curious look. Three teenaged boys, who certainly didn't need a nanny, came to the kitchen.'

' "Line up against the wall in order of size," I said, 'What are your names?'

They gave their names which I forgot immediately.

' "Go and get your ball. Then we can have a game of ball on your lawn and I can get to know you better."

' "I'm afraid your services are no longer required,' said their mother as if I had actually sexually assaulted the boys.

' "Why are my services no longer required? You haven't sampled them yet. Your attitude is distasteful."

' "I would like you to leave my house, now."

' "Don't worry, lady, I shall. Besides, your children are far too big to need a nanny, unless they are mentally retarded." '

Isabel laughed convulsively. 'Ellie, you're quite mad!' she said.

Bob started talking to me in Russian and it was fortunate that I had been brushing up the language for a month in anticipation of this occasion. We had a short conversation in Russian and I said I could only speak it perfectly if I was drunk.

I waited for him to roar with laughter which he did and I laughed with him. The other people in the room, including Isabel and her son, were left out.

I was determined to sit at Bob's table and went into the kitchen to talk to Betty. Lunch consisted of smoked salmon, caviare, cold chicken in a sauce, and strawberries.

Bob poured some vodka into his glass to drink with the caviare.

'May I have some, please?' I said.

'No. I can't give it to you as it will make you ill. You've already had several glasses of wine.'

'Go on, Bob, be a sport.'

'No. I categorically forbid it. You'll be ill.'

The Speed I had taken was beginning to wear off. I threw my napkin under the table as an excuse to get under the table to take some more.

When I got up, I noticed a Polish woman sitting next to Bob. She was slim, her long curly blonde hair was dishevelled and she wore a see-through white garment descending well into her cleavage. Her skirt was strategically raised and her sun-tanned legs were crossed and could be seen across the table. She tried to push me out of the conversation to get as much of Bob's attention as she could, speaking Polish.

I certainly wasn't going to have any of this and gave her one of my homicidal glares. I'm sure Betty, too, resented her presence and her brazen behaviour.

Bob was called to the telephone. Apparently Gorbachev was wishing him happy birthday.

I seized the opportunity to speak to the Polish woman when Bob was out of the room. I caught her eye and said 'For Christ's sake put your legs under the table and cover them with your skirt. This is a respectable residence, not a disorderly house. And another thing, stop monopolizing Bob's attention!'

When Bob returned, she talked to him incessantly but I constantly interrupted her.

'Bob, may I have a signed copy of Joe Haines's biography of you? It could be a late birthday present.'

'Yes, of course you can. I'll have it sent to you.' When was your birthday?'

'A month ago.'

'What date?'

'May 6th.'

Thereafter, Bob addressed everyone collectively about his experiences during the war. I revelled in his heroic exploits and stared at him throughout, hoping to catch his eye.

When lunch was over, I went to the marquee and watched another film about Bob's achievements before going home. That was one of the happiest days of my life.

Within a week, I received the book. Bob had even remembered when my birthday was. He had written in the book: 'To Eleanor, in friendship from Bob.'

I had just come back from a friend's funeral when the book reached me. I was overjoyed.

I stayed in his house again soon after but he wasn't there. When I came down the drive, I never looked at the pillars outside the house where he left his car, just in case the space was empty, meaning he was away.

I got out with my suitcase and rang the bell, now in low spirits because there was no car outside. I suddenly felt ill and exhausted. I had been suffering from insomnia for some months and hadn't slept so much as a minute that week.

Genius opened the door.

'Good evening. Is Mr Maxwell not at home?'

'No, Miss.'

'Do you know if he will be coming home tomorrow?'

'I don't know.'

'Is he ill?'

'I don't know anything about him, Miss.'

'Oh, I thought you worked for him.'

'Sometimes.'

'Where is he?'

'He could be anywhere, Miss.'

Then I understood that this man wasn't called 'Genius' for nothing. 'Mrs Maxwell's here, Miss,' he said. 'May I take your suitcase?'

'Thank you.'

I went in and the first thing I wanted was a stiff gin and tonic.

I found Bob's nephew and niece sitting in the living room. They were the children of Bob's charming and friendly sister, Sylvia Rosen, whom I had taken to see *A Clockwork Orange* in the early 70s. She never said whether she liked it or not. Sylvia's son, whose name I can't remember, was about 8 feet tall which is why Bob always referred to him as 'the dwarf'.

'Where's your uncle?' I asked the girl. 'Why isn't he here?'

'Don't ask me. I haven't the faintest idea where he is. I saw Ghislaine yesterday. She had a cold.'

I regarded this as unsolicited information.

I went to the bar and poured myself a socking great gin and tonic. I drank it in one go and a few minutes later, I felt more relaxed. Eventually, Betty came downstairs and I greeted her and gave her a box of chocolates for the house.

'Is Bob not well?' I asked calmly.

'Bob's fine. Unfortunately, he's had to stay at the *Mirror*. He's got very bad toothache and we're trying to get hold of a dentist.'

'I know a dentist called Russell King in Cavendish Square.' I quoted the phone number. But I'm not sure whether he practises at weekends.'

'Oh dear, oh dear!'

'What about ringing Talking Pages through the operator? They have a list of dentists which states whether they work at weekends. I'll ring them if you like.'

'That's very sweet of you. At the moment I could do with a drink. What will you have?'

'Perrier and ice, please.' (The gin was getting to my head.)

'I can see you live dangerously! Won't you have something stronger?'

'I won't, thanks.'

Genius came in to say dinner was ready. There was a rule in the house made by Bob that your conversation could be lewd and ribald if eating in the kitchen but it had to be clean in the dining-room. We ate in the dining-room. By the time I'd had a few glasses of wine, I felt much better.

'Are you writing another book?' asked Betty.

'Not yet,' I said. 'I've been in deadlock for 2 years.'

'Oh, you lazy old thing!'

The rest of the conversation took place between her and myself. The niece and nephew were subdued and silent.

Later, Betty took me down to the wine cellar. The walls on the stairs leading to the cellar were covered with photographs of Bob, including the heroic picture of Field Marshal Montgomery attaching the MC to his chest for his bravery on the field. This is a powerfully moving picture and I have a replica of it on my bedroom wall, together with other flattering pictures of Bob which, since his death, have cheered and comforted me.

There was another picture on the cellar stairs. Bob was standing on a bridge, wearing a beige overcoat, looking lovingly at the camera.

'That's beautiful,' I said. 'How I wish it were mine!'

Betty hurriedly took it down and placed it into my hands. I was mortified with embarrassment.

'I can't possibly take this lovely picture away from you. It would be terribly wrong. She was determined to give it to me and in return I wrote her a long letter of appreciation, and because my insomnia had caused me to have no sleep for a week, my mind wasn't quite what it should have been. I kept a copy of the letter and when I read it at a later date, I found it was pretty dotty.

In the cellar was a large cabinet adjacent to the bottles of wine. Betty got out a towering pile of photographs, mostly of Bob. She very kindly gave me all the photographs I found attractive.

When we'd finished in the cellar, she took me to her study and showed me about ten large leather-bound volumes full of press cuttings lovingly glued in. They went back to the days when publicity about him had started.

I thought what a rare and saintly lady she was and was profoundly moved by the trouble she took to show me all these things until 1.00 in the morning when she must have been exhausted. I felt at one with her and Bob's absence no longer troubled me. It was as if he were in the house.

I didn't sleep that night so I dressed and was down to breakfast in the kitchen at 8.30. Betty came down later and I got up and greeted her. She addressed me in French but my French had suffered appallingly because of the insomnia.

'How about all those dentists, Betty?'

'How kind of you to ask! I managed to get a dentist lined up late last night. He's going to the *Mirror* this morning.'

I said I was relieved. Genius brought me some fresh orange juice and gave a pile of newspapers to Betty. We sat and ate and read.

Later, I helped her wrap up Christmas presents and put a colossal pile of cards into envelopes. They appeared to be addressed to each citizen in every country in the world, including England, including myself and my father.

'Oh, I'll take those, Betty, there's no point in sending them out.'

This year's card was fairly low profile in appearance, showing the words Pergamon Press in gold letters against a blue background. Whenever I stayed with the Maxwells just before Christmas, I always took the cards for my father and myself.

I learnt through disagreeable experience. Every Christmas, guests came to our house. If Bob had his own picture on the card and it was unflattering, guests would take it down and pass it round the room, joking about it and exciting humorous comments.

'Look here, we're not having any Maxwell jokes in this house!' said my loyal father angrily.

Another guest took the card down the following year.

'Why does that man send his photograph out?' she said, unfortunately in my hearing.

I went menacingly up to her with a glass of neat whisky in my hand. I stood over her, glaring at her.

'What did you say?' I shouted.

Fear came into her voice and her face.

'I only asked why that man had to send his photograph out,' she said with extreme timidity.

'I'll tell you why! Because the person you call that man, whose picture you took from my father's mantelpiece to comment on it, has done nothing but heroic deeds all his life, as well as saving my own life and if you had done what he did you would probably send pictures of yourself out — that is, if you were prettier!'

I was taught a lesson. Every time I went to the Maxwells before Christmas, I would destroy the card to my father and whenever my father asked where it was, I explained that Betty was under too much pressure and would not be sending any cards out.

I rang Bob's office at the *Mirror* and asked if I could go round there to see him. He had often asked me to make a date to meet him there. One of his many secretaries, Andrea Martin, whom I suspected may possibly have had carnal relations with Bob, took my call. I later saw a photograph of both of them barefoot walking on a beach towards the sunset in some southern clime. This suggested to me that they might possibly have gone to bed afterwards and the jealousy I suffered was agonizing.

'Is it possible for Mrs Maxwell to be there too? I haven't seen her for a long time either,' I said.

'What do you want to speak to Mr and Mrs Maxwell about?' asked Andrea, startling me.

'Oh, just my usual interests, homosexual sado-porn, black rubber mackintoshes, whips, the Marquis de Sade, drugs, street-fights, necrophilia, flick-knives, that sort of thing.'

There was a pause at the other end of the line. I'll kill this woman if she's been crawling into bed with Bob, I thought. It also crossed my mind that if the rumour were true, it would be so discourteous to Betty if Andrea didn't ask her permission first.

'Are you really serious?' said Andrea. 'What do you want to talk to Mr Maxwell about?'

'I'm sure Mr Maxwell will tell you afterwards if he thinks you need to know. Would you please look for a free date in his diary without asking me any further questions. I hope I haven't offended you by speaking plainly.'

Andrea's tone became less brisk and more genial.

She named a date. 'He's free then but only for a late drink. Last time you rang you said you'd like to see the Mirror come off the presses. He'd love to show you but he has to go out afterwards.'

'That sounds fine by me. I'll make a note of that date. Sorry I cracked silly jokes earlier.'

'That's OK,' said Andrea. 'Mrs Maxwell will be coming to the Mirror that evening so you may easily see her too.'

I slept badly every night until I was due to go to the Mirror. I bought Bob some caviare and Betty some flowers. That day, I couldn't concentrate on my work at all. I went out to lunch but had no appetite. When I came back I spent my time pacing up and down. Later that afternoon, I had to take 20 mg of Valium. I left my office, forgetting to turn off the computer and as I wasn't due at the Mirror until later on, I went to the pub and got systematically drunk, smoked forty cigarettes and read James Hadley Chase.

The smell of whisky was on my breath but I knew from previous occasions that Bob never expressed disapproval of that unless the drinker happened to be working for him.

When I thought I was able to walk, I started my journey to the *Mirror*. It seemed like 300 miles because my snake skin boots (Bob's favourites) were agony. I also had on a pale green leather suit (he loved my leather suits).

I couldn't make the walk and got a taxi for the rest of the journey. I was jumpy and arrogant throughout the ride. The driver was pretty bad-tempered as well. We had a row and I got out refusing to pay him.

I was still early for Bob. I went to a pub just opposite Maxwell House in Fetter Lane. I swallowed three Speed and continued to read James Hadley Chase. Then I entered the building with a feeling of monumental euphoria.

'I'm to see Mr Maxwell,' I said to a guard behind a desk. He made a call to certify my presence was genuine and took me to the lift.

The ground floor looked immaculately clean but very ordinary. The lift ascended quietly and swiftly to the ninth floor. When it opened, I saw an entirely new world.

I am not an authority on interior decoration but the room I had been left in looked majestic and was wonderfully adorned with either seventeenth or eighteenth-century paintings on the walls — I'm not sure which. The furniture might have belonged to Kings and the carpets were embroidered with a spectacular letter M. With what I had consumed and taken, I felt like Dante ascending to the firmament to be re-united with Beatrice.

There was no one there to greet me but I didn't care. A huge window covering a wall reflected the whole of London. I had an urge to smoke but couldn't because Bob and Betty were averse to anyone smoking in front of them. This may have been due to Bob's diseased lung when he was in his 30s.

I grew restless and started walking round in circles. Eventually, I came to a chess set with intricately carved pieces. A game was in progress. I moved the pieces back to their original places and started a game with myself, walking backwards and forwards, quietly whistling *A Silent Crowd Gathered Outside of Kilmainham*.

A servant suddenly entered the room.

'You shouldn't have moved those men,' he said in a flustered, anxious voice. 'You have interrupted a game betweem Mr Maxwell and the Russian Ambassador.'

'Oh, dearie me!'

'Perhaps you would care for a drink?'

My breathing started to get alarmingly fast.

'Yes, please. I'll be having a double whisky if that's all right with you. Where's Mr Maxwell? He is here, isn't he?'

'Yes, he is here,' said the servant. 'He's expecting you but he's still in his office. I really would thank you not to touch his chessmen. They are his pride and joy.'

'I won't touch them, Scout's honour,' I said.

Eventually Betty came in, splendidly attired. She explained she had to go out to dinner.

We had a long talk about the lives of each of her children whom she said were all very happy with the exception of one of them who had a depressive illness.* She talked at length about Bob whom she said was working too hard and causing her great concern.

'But with Bob, work is play,' I said. 'When he works, he's like a child playing with his toys. Surely it must be good for him. If he stopped, he'd go off his head.'

'I hope you're right. Ghislaine bought a beautiful dress in Paris last week.' She described the dress at length. My breathing started going wrong again.

'You are all right, aren't you?' she asked.

'Yes. Has Ghislaine got another man?'

'Yes, she's been going out with him for some time now.' She gave his name which was of such incredible length it could have covered the front page of a tabloid newspaper.

'Does Bob like him?'

'No. There's a big problem here. He can't stand him.'

'Do you know why?'

'He's Italian and Bob has a pathological loathing for Italians.'

'Why?'

'I don't really know. Part of it is that he thinks they're all drunken idiots.'

We talked for a few more minutes until she said she had to go. I gave her her flowers which delighted her. We kissed goodbye.

'You won't have to wait much longer now. One of the secretaries will take you into Bob as soon as he's ready.'

I knew the heinous consequences of smoking in front of Bob. A woman ushered me into a lavish hallway with magenta velvet chairs where she said I could smoke provided I put the cigarette out as soon as Bob came out of his office. My heart was going frighteningly fast because of the Speed — so much so that I could hear it. There were quite a few

* I do not wish to name this person.

boring looking women up there, all dressed in pretty boring-looking uniforms.

I asked one of the women to give me a copy of the *Mirror* and started doing the crossword.

In 10 minutes, Bob came out. He gave me a hug and a kiss on the mouth. He took me into his American-style, spacious office and I was surprised to see he had all the blinds drawn and the lights out except for a small Anglepoise lamp on his desk.

'You're looking more beautiful by the minute,' he said.' I like the sexy leather.'

I said nothing. I smiled radiantly and rolled my eyes at him.

'I've brought you some of your favourite *Beluga*' I said, giving him the caviare. He was overtly grateful and he gave me another kiss, this time on the forehead.

'There's something worrying you, isn't there?' he said suddenly. 'Come on, let's have it.'

I had an obsession about one of the women who worked with me. I hated her guts at the time and lay awake at night thinking of ways to kill her, although I get on perfectly well with her now and we are on reasonably friendly terms.

Her name is Joyce Larby. I had been at the hospital for 3 years and was highly regarded. Joyce Larby, on the other hand, was only an agency temp. The Administrator, a rugger-playing Welshman, called us all in without warning and told us that Joyce was being promoted over my head to the rank of Line Manager. Doris (my best friend in the hospital, and the epitome of loyalty and discretion) and I would have lunch together every day and fantasize about murdering Joyce.

I told Bob the whole story.

He leant his head on one side and raised his eyebrows in his famous quizzical expression as if to say 'you bloody fool!'

'Now, why on earth did you allow Joyce Larby to do that?'

'It was all done behind my back, blast it! It was engineered behind closed doors like a *coup*.'

Bob chewed on his unlit cigar.

'And what is our Eleanore going to do to get rid of Joyce Barby?'

'Larby,' I corrected. 'There's nothing I can do at this stage but if she hots up, I'll call the Branch Secretary of NALGO in.'

Bob swivelled on his chair.

'I have an important proposition to make to you.'

'What would that be?'

'Chuck Joyce Barby altogether.'

'Larby.'

'Larby, Barby, call her what you will! Do you know what I'm trying to say to you?'

'As a matter of fact, no.'

'I'm asking you if you'd like to come and work for me at the *Mirror*. When I offered you a job 20 years ago, you turned me down. Perhaps this time, you'll say 'yes'.'

I had a yearning for a cigarette and was just about to get one out but checked myself.

'I'm very honoured and touched by your offer and ashamed to have to turn it down. I'm afraid I will only ever work in hospitals. I like the hustle and bustle of bestethoscoped, white-coated men rushing down corridors and the perpetual toing and froing of stretchers borne by sweating porters. I like the smells in hospitals. They remind me of my school.'

Bob looked pretty aghast.

'You can't fool me,' he said jocularly. 'I've known you since you were little more than a puppy. You like the stench of death and decay. You love the blood and guts. Don't think I don't know about all this. I read that book you wrote about me, remember?'

I was intensely embarrassed. I longed for a cigarette more than anything else in the world. I looked around the room still curious as to why the blinds were drawn and the lights turned off.

'I'll tell you what, Bob. I will work for you on one condition and one condition only.'

'Which is what?'

'That you train to become a doctor and later a consultant surgeon, wearing a dazzling white coat in plush rooms in Harley Street and having an array of swivelling, leather-studded chairs and a swish leather studded couch.'

'Christ, you're barmy! Come with me and I'll show you the *Mirror*.'

When we got outside the strangely dark room, I noticed Bob much more fully in the glaring lights shining from the ceiling.

I had absolutely no idea he was dying of emphysema and multiple impairment of the brain. Nor did I know that in only a few months, his thinking processes would deteriorate to such a terrifying degree that no one would dare go near him. Every time I rang his office during the last months of his life, excuses were made that he was living in America.

I also had no idea that this was the last time I would ever see him.

I observed him closely under the glaring lights. I had never seen him look so attractive since he was young. He had lost some weight and his thick black hair was slightly dishevelled. Added to this, the top two buttons of his shirt were undone and his tie was loosened which set my blood on fire. The only thing that struck me as strange was the fact that his glistening black eyes failed to focus on an object for more than one split second at a time. I held his hand as we descended in the lift to the office occupied by his editors.

As we entered their office, the editors, who all had nice, smiling faces, jumped to their feet. The scene was akin to Beatrice showing Dante the firmament. Bob said what he always did when introducing me. He said I joined the Communist Party, taught myself Russian and went to Russia alone. I was beginning to find these words soporific. The editors looked baffled. I questioned them at length about their previous employment as Bob stood beside me.

'What story are you running?' Bob asked one of these decent, well-mannered, wholesome-looking editors.

'We're covering the actress (sorry, readers, I've forgotten her name) who has become a born-again Christian.'

'A fine story,' said Bob. 'It's never too late to turn to God.'

'Oh, most assuredly, Mr Maxwell!' said the Editor.

Bob had already given me more whisky and my mood was now completely euphoric but my mind was sluggish and on the point of being puerile. What a wonderful sight to see this handsome, god-like Napoleonic colossus surrounded by his soldiers.

I got a bit out of control.

'Do you personally cover stories about harassment in hospitals?' I asked the Editor in a booming voice two octaves lower than its ordinary pitch.

Bob put his hand on my shoulder.

'Now, we're not going to discuss that woman, Joan Barby in here.'

'Joyce Larby.'

'Never mind what her bloody name is! Come and meet Mr Whittaker who is our Royal Correspondent.'

I shook Mr Whittaker's hand and smiled but to this day I shall never remember what he looked like.

Then Bob, bigger and taller than his editors, addressed them collectively as they all remained standing, reluctant to return to their desks.

'Do you know that I've just offered Eleanore a job on the *Mirror*?'

'Indeed, Mr Maxwell?' said the Editor running the story on the born-again Christian. 'And do you know she's turned my offer down for a second time, the cheeky little miss!'

'I'm sorry to hear that,' said the Editor, lowering his head as if someone had died.

'She prefers to work in hospitals,' because she's obsessed by death, said Bob.' She only likes to be in places where there's plenty of blood and guts. She hangs about outside mortuaries waiting for hearses to turn up, the morbid pussycat.'

The Editor cleared his throat.

'He's only joking,' I said.

I then shook hands again with the editors who maintained their angelic smiles. Bob took me to see the *Mirror* coming off the presses.

When I accounted this wonderful experience to Nicky and likened the smiling editors to the characters in *Paradiso*, he said I was completely mad.

'Don't you realize they were all terrified of Maxwell?' he said.

When the *Mirror* came off the presses, they made an unbroken rhythmic noise as they moved from one level to another.

I was hypnotized by them. I saw before me a river of volcanic lava sent by the gods in colours of red and white, purifying the earth with the waves of the sea, the fleece of freshly-shorn lambs and newly-fallen snow.

Beside me, stood the giant, velvet, black bear, taking me by the hand. A Christian might have likened this to the Second Coming.

I stood engrossed as the wonderful spectacle unfolded before me and as I averted my eyes to the big, noble, black bear, I wept.

'Have you got a car?' asked Bob when he'd shown me the presses.

'No. There's nowhere to park in London.'

'That's no problem. I'll get one of my drivers to take you home!'

'That's very kind of you. Are you sure?'

'Stop saying I'm kind. Yes of course I'm sure.'

A car drew up in the yard. The driver later told me he had driven Ghislaine to represent her father at Marjorie Proops's husband's funeral.

I hugged Bob and kissed him goodbye, again on the mouth. It is horrifying to think that I had no idea I would never see him again.

'Goodbye, Missy and thank you for my prezzie. Do try and get away from all this blood and guts, and stop hanging around outside mortuaries.'

'I'll try, Bob. Thank you so much for taking the time to show me round the *Mirror*.'

Amidst the tragedy of my tale, I have a comical story to tell regarding

Marjorie Proops.

After Bob's death, there was prurient speculation about women going to bed with him; sometimes I saw it in the press, sometimes on the television. In each event, both jealousy and curiosity ate into me like a cancer.

I also read that Bob had frequently addressed Mrs Proops as 'my darling little daughter'.

I couldn't really imagine Bob taking this woman to his bed but my obsession was such that I was prepared to believe anything. One morning, after pacing up and down the room, a demon got into me and made me ring Mrs Proops at the *Mirror*.

'Mrs Proops. You've got to help me. I'm possessed. I wrote to you several times but got no reply (a lie). Please, you've got to help me.'

Mrs Proops voice was quite plummy. Her brogue could have been one of many London accents. She answered but her tone was unfriendly. I came straight out with it.

'Mrs Proops — I must know — when Robert Maxwell kissed you, was it on the cheek or on the mouth?'

'I find you most impertinent. Who are you?'

'My name's Natalie Klein. I'm not being rude but I *must* know.'

'You *are* being rude, bloody rude. What exactly do you want? Robert Maxwell was a very affectionate man.'

I began to breathe heavily.

'When you say he was an 'affectionate man', does that mean he used to beckon you into dark corners and put his hand between your legs?'

'Do you mind, Mrs Klein!' it must have been curiosity which prevented her hanging up.

'Please! You've got to help me!' I pleaded. I struggled to find words. Eventually they came to me.

'Mrs Proops, you do have a most unusual face and jaw-line, so much so that you might be attractive in the eyes of certain men. Perhaps your individual teeth and smile would appear unique and intriguing enough to cause Mr Maxwell to request that you gave him a blow job.'

Still the woman failed to hang up. Finally, she channelled her rage into one livid shout.

'GET OFF MY LINE!'

* * *

SOME TIME LATER

It was beginning to get dark on the afternoon of Tuesday, 5 November, 1991. Noreen Creedon, my Irish colleague and I were in our office busy with our computers. Noreen was quite a fiery woman and very pretty. I had a love-hate relationship with her although we were good friends most of the time.

We were taking a break. I was in a good mood and rolled up balls of paper and flicked them towards her. In retaliation she sang a song she knew I hated. It was a very dour, upsetting 1960s' song called *Blowing in the Wind*.

'For Christ's sake, stop singing that horrible morbid song!' I shouted. The telephone rang.

'You'll be answering that,' I said, 'as a penalty for singing that song!'

'But it's your turn to answer.'

'Answer that phone!' I said peremtorily.

A voice on the other end of the line asked to speak to me. The caller was my brother, Adrian. I took the call.

'Hullo.' I could tell by the tone of his voice that he was bringing me bad tidings. I got alarmed.

'Is everything all right?' I said, thinking illogically that such words would put right whatever he was going to tell me.

'No. I'm afraid I have some rather startling news for you.'

'Has someone in the family had an accident? Is someone ill?' I shouted.

This was inconveniencing Noreen who wanted to get her work finished in time to go to a fireworks party with her man — a funny form of celebration for an Irish woman, and a green one that, to attend, I thought.

'I'm afraid it's about Robert Maxwell,' said Adrian. 'I'm telling you now, before you go out and see it on the news-stands.'

My immediate reaction was of relief that no one in my family had been hurt but my hysteria mounted quickly on fearing that harm had come to Bob.

'Bob? Is he still alive?' I screamed.

'I'm afraid he's gone missing.'

'Gone missing? Gone missing? Missing from what?'

'The news has just come in from *Reuters*. He was on his boat, the *Ghislaine* and went to bed last night. He got up during the night and went out on to the deck. This morning, a search party was sent out when

98

he wasn't in his room and he wasn't anywhere to be found. He must either have accidentally fallen from the boat into the sea or committed suicide. He was in severe debt. That could be a motive for suicide.'

The telephone receiver was shaking in my hand.

'Of course he couldn't have fallen into the sea,' I said. Nor could he possibly have taken his life. The man would never ever have taken his life. It wouldn't be his style. The *Ghislaine* is a very big boat.' I was saying this to console myself rather than to accept reality. 'Just because someone can't be found it doesn't mean they're not there. He's probably in the lavatory.'

I could tell by my brother's voice that my efforts not to accept the truth were distressing him because he was certain poor Bob had drowned during the night and he felt it was his responsibility as a loving brother to make me believe it.

'No. The lavatories have been searched.'

'But it would take a week to search all the lavatories. I should imagine there are about eighty-four lavatories on that boat! Besides, if one of the lavatories happened to be locked, no crew-member would dare bang on the door if the Captain could have been on the other side of it.'

'No,' said my brother, 'every lavatory has been searched. I'm afraid he's been drowned.'

'How could he have done that by accident? He was murdered!' I shouted.

I began to feel extremely ill and fell off my chair and lost consciousness.

I woke up to hear Noreen shouting down the line. The shock had made me amnesic.

'Who are you shouting at? What's going on?'

It didn't take me long to realize the situation.

'You should never have rung your sister up! You should have come here and told her face to face! You're very irresponsible.'

'Don't speak to my brother like that,' I said feebly. 'Don't shout at him. He hasn't done any harm.'

I took the receiver.

'Why don't you get in a taxi and come round to the *Telegraph*,' said Adrian.

'Is there any whisky there?' I asked urgently.

'Yes, yes, plenty of whisky. Come on over.'

Noreen wanted to go and watch the fireworks so she rang Doris (my closest friend at work) and told her the sad news. Doris, forever faithful, came immediately.

Some of the doctors were coming into the office to check their results before doing medical reports. One of the Senior House Officers, Melanie Shaw, was supportive and held my hand.

Doris told her what had happened.

'I think I need to get out of here,' I said.

Doris and Melanie helped me outside.

'You'll get a taxi, won't you?' said Melanie.

'No. Doris and I are going out for a drink. Would you like to come with us?'

'I can't,' said Melanie. 'I've got to get back to the ward to see a patient.'

'Thank-you so much for helping me down,' I said, 'I won't forget this.'

Doris kindly bought me a considerable amount of whisky in the *Red Lion* across the road. The whisky released the grief. I began to sob loudly while a nice man at the bar kindly, if somewhat unwisely, bought me even more. Readers of the *Evening Standard* quietly read their papers, sometimes rattling them in the air to get to the inner pages. The headlines kept flashing in front of my eyes, lashing them with acid.

MAXWELL DEAD;
MAXWELL DIES AT SEA;
MAXWELL IS DROWNED.

* * *

At home there had been a lot of serious confusion due to the crass stupidity of the afternoon caretaker whose name was Len. I rang up this cretin of a man from the *Red Lion* to tell my man friend whom I shall refer to as H, that Robert Maxwell had been drowned and I told him to go up and tell H the tragic news straight away so that I would not have to tell him myself.

I also told him that Doris's husband, a singularly eccentric man, who always dressed as a skiing instructor and was known as 'Napoleon' because of his uncanny resemblance to the Emperor, would be going to the flat long before Doris and I returned and I told him specifically to let Napoleon in.

When I made this call in the crowded pub with Doris at my side, I had already had too much to drink and I was hysterical but by no means incoherent. I did not realize quite how loudly I was shouting but Doris told me later that I had reduced the room to silence.

I first rang Headington Hill Hall (calmly) to tell Betty how deeply shocked and horrified I was. Her secretary, Jay Miller, told me in a shaking voice that Betty and Philip (her oldest surviving son) had already flown to Tenerife to identify Bob. Then I ran out of coins.

When I rang the caretaker of the building I lived in, he refused to accept the charge. I rang him three or four times, giving my surname with which he appeared unfamiliar. He still refused. If I'd had a gun, I probably would have gone round and shot him.

Doris efficiently got some change from the flabbergasted barman. 'She's talking to a man who's totally deaf and she's been cut off,' she said adroitly.

I rang the caretaker and asked him what the hell he meant by refusing to accept my calls and accompanied my tirade by the most horrible language . I also told him I would report him and have him removed from his post. He must have been holding the receiver a yard away from his ear.

'Listen very, very carefully,' I shouted. 'If you can't remember what I say, write it down.'

'Yes, Miss Berry.'

'Two things: First, Robert Maxwell has been drowned. Have you understood that and written it down?'

'Who's Robert Maxwell?' asked the criminally half-witted man. 'Is he a resident here?'

'No. You will find a man in my flat to whom you will break the news I have just given you. Just repeat my words.'

'I'm to go and find a man upstairs and tell him Michael Jackson has been bound over.'

To this day, I have no idea what I bellowed to this man, who was one of these proverbial, walking Einsteins, except that I thought my tonsils were bleeding. I had to repeat the sad news several times before the man got it right.

'Now, there's a second thing: A man called Napoleon, who dresses like a skiing instructor, will be coming to this address shortly. You are to let him in and send him upstairs. Repeat these two messages, please.'

The caretaker appeared more confused than ever.

'A man was drowned and another man will be collecting Napoleon for his skiing lesson.'

I couldn't say anything further. My spirit had been broken by the caretaker's calculated obtuseness. The barman came over to Doris, asking her to take me outside.

It was some way to the Isle of Dogs where the *Telegraph* had been moved to. The whisky made me horrifyingly manic. I started to sing *For Those in Peril on the Sea* followed by *The Wearing of the Green*. The manic attack was infectious. Doris started singing as well. The taxi driver put cotton wool into his ears and closed his window.

Adrian, my brother, forever fiercely kind, loving and loyal, was in the lobby to meet us. I wasn't really aware of my surroundings. The effect of the whisky had partly worn off. I rushed towards my brother, threw my arms round his neck and sobbed hysterically. Although full of pity and brotherly love, he became confused and wasn't sure how to handle the situation. He suggested driving Doris and me back to my flat.

My brother went home. I let myself and Doris in where H and Napoleon in his skiing clothes were waiting. I can't remember a thing about this small gathering except for the fact that Napoleon was nervously eating large quantities of biscuits. It was like a dream. Napoleon and Doris left after about half an hour. I then told H about the tragedy as the half-witted caretaker had failed to take the message.

I have no knowledge at all of what happened after Doris's and Napoleon's departure. Apparently, I had gone to the bathroom where I had a very serious accident concerning my arm. H rang 999 and I was ambulanced off to the Westminster Hospital and thence to another nicer hospital where there was a microsurgery unit in which surgeons could sew on severed limbs and probably even severed heads.

I refused to have a general anaesthetic because I feel ill for days afterwards if I do. I also prefer a local so that I can see what's going on and talk to the surgeons about my books.

'Miss Berry,' said the Consultant sharply, 'if you say one more word about the contents of your books, you are going to lose your arm.'

Following the operation, I was taken to a ward to be shared with three other women. It was bed-time and the Ward Sister was handing out sleeping pills. She passed them from one patient to another in a tiny plastic cup. She came to me last.

'What is this drug?' I asked, looking at a small yellow, egg-shaped capsule.

'Temazepam.'

'I'm very sorry but Temazepam belongs to the Benzodiazopine family. It is highly addictive. When Dr Ratner my GP came to see one of the nurses here today, he gave her instructions for me to take the sleeping pills he had arranged to have specially flown in from Paris.'

'Ere! 'Ark at Lady Muck!' shouted a woman of about my age, but

102

who looked much older, of course and whose bed was in the nicest part of the ward by the window with a spectacular view of London.

I ignored her. I was more preoccupied with getting my sleeping pills.

'It's Temazepam or nothing,' said the nurse.

'In that case, would you please bring the telephone in so that I can ring Dr Ratner?'

'Not a chance, I'm afraid. It's too late at night for telephones to be brought onto the ward.'

'All right,' I said, 'would you please ring him from a telephone outside.'

The nurse lost her temper

'This is not an amusement centre. We've got other things to do! You're not the only patient here!'

I didn't like her attitude at all. I started shouting.

'First, my taxes pay for patients to be treated kindly in hospitals. Second, this sort of duty comes within your job description, advocating courtesy and flexibility. Third, you could get a Final Written Warning for being uncooperative with patients. I've taken your name from your lapel and when I leave, I shall report you to the Head of Medical Personnel.' I gave her Ratty's number.

She had been gone for 10 minutes.

'Sorry, there's only an answering service.' That meant she wouldn't get consent for anything from half an hour to 3 hours. At least she had the courage to face me with this news.

'I regret, I can't give you your pills from Paris. You're not written up for them.'

The words 'written up' uttered to me by nurses in all the hospitals I've been in, produce an allergy reaction. When I hear them, I fly into a rage.

I grabbed the unsympathetic, uncaring woman by her uniform, with my undamaged arm.

'Have you any idea how I came to be here?' I bellowed. 'Do you realize whose death I am mourning?'

'I don't know and I don't care!' said the nurse.

'Oh, don't you? I'm mourning one of our major national heroes, a man who, with the help of Sir Winston Churchill, won the last war single-handed when Field Marshal Montgomery personally attached the MC to his chest. A man who brought relief to famines in Third World countries. A man who gave bread to the starving, hope to the despairing and work to the jobless. Even heads of state rang him day and night for advice before they made decisions of global significance. And I can go on...'

'Oh, please don't,' pleaded the nurse.

By this time, I was laughing nervously and the laughter soon turned to tears.

'If you make any more noise,' I shall have to send for the Duty Psychiatrist,' said the nurse.

'I don't need a bloody psychiatrist!' I screamed. 'All I want are my pills from Paris. Then you will be blessed with the silence you crave.'

"Course you needs a bloomin' psychiatrist, Lady Muck,' remarked the odious woman in the bed by the window.

I ignored her and directed my energy towards the nurse.

'I'll make a bargain with you, nurse,' I said, 'If you bring me my pills, I'll go straight to sleep and be as silent as a sedated ant. If you do not, I shall lie on my back until the sun rises and I shall sing Irish rebel songs so loudly that the noise will reverberate all over this hospital and probably all the way down the street.'

'Sorry, you haven't been "written up",' was her sole reaction to this threat.

'All right, if that's how you feel, I shall be obliged to open fire. Do you stand ready to receive my fire?'

'Ain't she pompous!' Again it was the mad woman by the window. 'Pompous as well as flippin' barmy!'

Date boxes, bananas, grapes and other objects were pelted in my direction.

The war had begun. I lay flat on my back. I started off with *The Death of Kevin Barry* which I sang to the tune of *Clementine* repeating one of the verses several times over:

'Kevin Barry, do not leave me.
Kevin Barry, do not die.'
Cried his broken-hearted mother
When she saw the gibbet high.

There were angry shouts of 'Oh, do shut up!' accompanied by expletives. How I wished Bob were there to witness the scene! He had always gone round telling people that I was 'one hell of a feisty woman.' He would have loved it particularly as I was releasing my grief in his memory.

I sang another black-humoured song with each verse ending with the words: *Ah, me coople of sticks of gelig-i-nite and me old alarum clock.*

I suddenly realized that Nicky (my other brother) had very kindly brought me two bottles of claret which I had hidden under my bed. Using one arm, I opened one by pushing the cork down into the bottle. I drank a large quantity of it and as a result became even more manic.

I knew another Irish song with an attractive tune but only knew a few words of it.

'On the scaffold, died Patrick Murphy
In another fight for the Green again.'

By now, some hours had passed. The wine helped me sing even more loudly. I saw nothing of the nurse. I sang the above words over and over again. It was 4.00 in the morning and despite the noise, the other patients had gone to sleep on their Temazepam.

I heard the nurse's voice on the telephone across the corridor. Her tone was curt and crisp.

'Mrs Cullen, will you please come and take your sister away from this hospital.'

The timing of the call must have terrified Harriet. She probably thought I had died from some unknown cause and that she was being asked to identify me.

I listened, waiting for the nurse to speak again.

'I'm sorry, Mrs Cullen but your sister is causing a major breach of the peace and is on the verge of bringing this hospital to a complete standstill. She is the rowdiest, stubbornest, most disorderly and most difficult patient I have ever had to deal with in my entire nursing career.'

Then she came in to see me.

'I'm afraid we really can't tolerate incidents of this nature in this hospital. Your sister will be collecting you in about 20 minutes.'

'Do you mean you rang her up at 4.00 in the bloody morning and disturbed her entire household?'

'I had no choice,' said the nurse.

'You had no choice! You had no choice! You've no business disturbing other people's sleep at this hour of the night. Have you no respect for a person's need to get a decent night's sleep? A person who wakes people in the night is a selfish person.'

'You smell of drink,' said the nurse provocatively.

'Yes, I know I do. Robert Maxwell's dead.'

She showed the first and only sign of compassion towards me.

'I had no idea you were a friend of his. I saw it on the news, of course. I'm so sorry.'

Soon, Harriet appeared. I felt enormously guilty for having caused her sleep to be disturbed, and she was very tolerant about it. Had I been her, I would have blown my top and refused to come. She didn't seem concerned that her sleep had been disturbed. Instead, she was terrified I was going to be sick.

'Is my sister going to be sick?' she asked urgently, pinning the already grossly traumatized nurse against the wall.

'I don't know, Mrs Cullen,' she spluttered. 'She's had a lot to drink. Apparently, your brother, Nicholas, brought some bottles in and your sister drank them.'

Harriet, my sister, is a very sturdy old soul. Her nerves are excellent but like all Berrys, including myself, she is prone to occasional, short-lived outbursts of temper. She is generous, kindly, compassionate, hospitable, friendly and sensitive to the feelings of others.

She is married to Martin Cullen (pronounced Martine Coozhen) a delightful, extremely jolly (on the surface) Argentinian psychoanalyst who is an intellectual and prone to what I suspect to be quite unpleasant episodes of melancholia. He has a saucy sense of humour, a kind heart and a quirky, amusing way of speaking English. For example, he sometimes refers to widows as 'windows' and mortuaries as 'dead-houses' with the stress on 'house'. He has always been kindly towards me and came and comforted me in the hospital.

Harriet never panics in a crisis as I do. There is just one thing that nauseates, terrifies and repulses her to the point of considerably dramatic hysteria and that is the possibility of someone being sick.

Even as a child, she was known to fling herself screaming from cars travelling up to 60 m.p.h. when someone had been sick in them. On one of these occasions, when I, 5 years her junior, suffered from car-sickness, she hurled herself into a nearby field and broke her leg. Harriet is a brunette and I am a blonde.

'Be honest with me,' she said urgently as she continued to pull me to my feet as I kept falling over in the corridor, singing 'For Those In Peril on the Sea,' 'is there any risk at all that you're going to be sick?'

'No, no.'

'It was naughty of Nicky to bring you all that drink. If you are sick, I'm going to be livid with him and I'm going to take you straight to his house.'

'I'm *not* going to be sick!'

Harriet and Martin looked after me for a few days and kept me occupied with visits to the cinema. In the evenings, I played with my puppy-like nephews, Miguel and Mingo, then aged 9 and 7. Harriet was anxious not to let me out of the house.

'Why?' I asked.

'Because in your present state, I wouldn't put it past you to take a taxi round to the offices of the *Sun* newspaper and slit someone's throat with a carving knife.'

I was able to laugh for the rest of the day at this remark.

Opposite Harriet's kitchen, across a stretch of grass, is a house occupied by a team of high-flying, energetic homosexuals. They spend a lot of time in a lavatory with a wall-to-wall, uncurtained window. Whenever they get up from the lavatory, they never use any paper and take it in turns to sit down.

Harriet keeps a large amount of claret in her kitchen. It amused me very much to open a bottle and watch these dotty men.

Harriet came in.

'What do you mean by drinking at 9.00 in the morning, so soon after you had hepatitis? Anyone would think you wanted to get cirrhosis of the liver like so many of the alcoholics on the Smith and Berry side of the family!'

'I was just coming down to look at the men before breakfast.' As I spoke I caught one of them by the eye and waved.'

Harriet was acutely embarrassed.

'Don't do that! I have to *live* here!'

After breakfast, I read the papers. Reading about Bob, before the Press turned on him, comforted me.

The next day I had to see Peter Rohde, the shrink. I didn't like having to do this at all. There were times when it upset me to talk about Bob and this was one of them. I was so distressed on my way to Rohde's rooms that I told the taxi driver to stop outside an off-licence where I bought a bottle of whisky. I was early so I asked the driver to take a longer route so that I could consume enough to put me at my ease.

I don't know what it feels like to have a heroin injection but the degree of euphoria I experienced drinking a large amount of whisky was about as enormous as that of someone who had just been injected. I was as manic as I was when my first book came out when I sat on the steps of the Cenotaph in Whitehall and sang all night, accompanied by two drunken Communists.

The driver waited for about 2 hours after leaving me in Harley Street. I had forgotten Rohde's door number and entered a building a few doors up, wearing one of Robert Maxwell's shirts which kept out the harsh

November wind far more than a fur coat.

The building was architecturally the same shape as the one containing Rohde's rooms and each room was identically situated. The equivalent of Rohde's room was on the right just inside the door.

I went in without ceremony with my left arm in a sling holding the bottle of whisky and a copy of the *Daily Mirror* under my right arm. I wore a black leather suit beneath the shirt and matching peak cap.

The man I faced was bending over a patient but when he saw me he sprang to his feet. He was too startled to ask who I was. In the end it transpired he was a dentist but I was too befuddled to know this. He was about 5 feet tall, wore outmoded black-rimmed glasses and was as bald as a billiard ball.

'Are you Peter Rohde, the psychiatrist?'

'Do I look like a psychiatrist?'

'I suppose so. You have to be certified insane before you're allowed to practise as a psychiatrist.'

A pause ensued while the dentist gathered what wits he could. His patient, an elderly woman with tight white curls, leaned timidly round from her supine chair, her mouth gaping open in horror and amazement.

'Who are you?' the dentist eventually managed to splutter.

My manic state had dramatically increased.

'You ask me who I am? There is no other Messiah but Robert Maxwell and you have the honour to be addressing his hallowed prophet!' I shouted.

The dentist looked as if a poisonous snake were crawling up his overalls towards his throat. His patient assumed the same gaping-mouthed pose.

'I order you to prostrate yourself on the floor and kiss the hallowed sleeve of my sacred garment!' I held out my hand with the sleeve extending a yard over it.

The dentist did not do what I asked him to which in the circumstances, was hardly surprising.

'Are you daring to disobey a prophet's orders?'

The dentist continued to look aghast.

I held the front page of the *Daily Mirror* in front of his face.

'Kiss the front page of this sacred newspaper!' I shouted.

The dentist turned away from me and turned on the drill. This was something I didn't care for at all.

'Turn that horrible thing off immediately. It's giving me toothache! Not only that, I spoke to you about this newspaper I have here. It was born of our Holy Messiah whose prophet you have the honour to stand in front of. Fling yourself to the floor and lick the front page, just as a dog licks its master!'

To my immense surprise, the dentist actually spoke. He had a delicate upper class accent and an unusually quiet, refined voice.

'Will you go away, please,' he said.

On my way out, I was accosted by the receptionist. She was about 45, quite obscenely fat for a woman, and looked like a grey, flabby indiarubber. She touched me heavily on my free arm.

'Get out of here and don't ever come back!'

'Do you realize I am mourning the Messiah's death? And while you're at it, kindly refrain from touching me.'

'Who are you referring to?' she said disagreeably.

'The late Robert Maxwell,' I said in a low voice.

'So you're mourning that evil bastard, are you? No wonder you need to see a psychiatrist!'

I raised my right arm, intending to inflict as much pain on her as I could but, even in my present state, I knew it would be an awful bore to get arrested so I used my tongue instead.

'Madam, you are *the* ugliest woman I've ever seen in my life. If there happened to be a grey, flabby indiarubber in here, I wouldn't be able to tell the difference between the two of you. Why don't you go and jump in a lake and if you can't find one lake big enough to hold you, go and jump in two bloody lakes!'

The great lump of lard had spoken ill of Bob. Once composed, I wrote a letter of complaint to the consultant neurologist who employed her. Ratty also went round at my request to talk to her employer. I shall never know to this day whether she is still working there.

Rohde was standing waiting for me in the street. He looked as if he had left his entire family in a burning house.

'Have you killed anyone, Miss Berry?' he said in his high-pitched voice.

'No, of course not, you big dope. Do you think I wish to share a cell with three repulsive lesbians?'

I was none too sober because of my grief. Rohde got hold of my right arm.

'I can walk without assistance, thank you.'

The consulting room used by Rohde was extremely dingy. I could tell immediately that he had borrowed it from some other doctor. Books on urology lay on occasional tables. Photographs of a hunt adorned the mantelpiece.

'What actually happened between you and that woman?'

'Oh, I insulted her, that's all, because she spoke ill of Bob.'

'What did you say to her?' asked Rohde, a tall, blonde fellow with blue eyes, boringly untarnished by vice. He could'nt pronounce his Rs and was a shy, timid left-winger who was polite and genial in a phlegmatic, pacifist sort of way.

I repeated my words.

'Don't you think that was offensive?'

'How could it be offensive if the fat bitch spoke ill of Bob?'

I took my seat in his dour consulting room and lit a cigarette. I was very shaky and had difficulty speaking. Silence reigned for 10 minutes.

'What's the point of this silence?' I asked. 'We're wasting time. Why don't you ask the questions and I'll give the answers?'

'Very well. Did you know he'd been ill?'

At the time, I was unaware that Bob had been ill. It was only later that Betty told me that he had so much fluid in his one remaining lung that the oxygen supply to his brain was diminishing day by day until he was no longer responsible for his actions.

'He was never ill,' I said bitterly. 'He was murdered. Some bastard pushed him and if I ever catch up with the murderer, I'll gouge out his eyes and cut his balls off!'

'Tell me about the accident you had,' he asked.

'I don't see the point. It bears no relevance to the case.'

'Oh, doesn't it?'

'I've just told you it doesn't so there's an end to it.'

My euphoria was beginning to wear off. I got out my bottle of whisky and took a couple of swigs. For the rest of the discussion I wept uncontrollably and said nothing. Then I fell unconscious to the floor and that's all I can remember.

I received a letter from Rohde accompanied by a bill.

Dear Miss Berry,
Please do not drink in my consulting room. I've got a bad back and if there were no-one on the premises, it would mean I'd have to carry you out.'

I wrote back a humorous letter which he did not find amusing.

Dear Dr Rohde,
Do you think Rhett Butler had a bad back when he carried Scarlett O'Hara from the flames of Atlanta?'

I didn't see him again although I think he's pretty good at his trade.

Later that week, I went out to lunch by myself in an Italian restaurant. A rare November ray of sun shone through the window I was sitting by, warming my right ear and the right side of my face. The restaurant was empty which relieved me because I wanted to be alone, savouring the sun and thinking about Bob. I ordered chicken and peas and gin and tonic.

An unkempt parson strolled into the room and to my horror, he came to my table.

'Do you mind if I accompany you?'

This man had interrupted the only period of peace I'd had since Bob died. I hated the idea of someone imposing themselves on my solitude.

'Yes, I mind very much,' I said. 'Every other table in here is free. Your clothing is off-putting and I passionately want to be alone. I am grieving.'

The parson increased my awkwardness.

'If you give me that person's name, we can sit here and pray together.'

'You are harassing me.' I shouted. 'I am not religious and I specifically want to be alone. Piss off!'

The waiter came to the table. 'I've brought you your usual, Sir, steak, spinach and chips. My order came immediately afterwards.

'I'm going to say grace,' said the parson. 'You don't mind, do you?'

'If you choose to indulge in your eccentricities, I wish you'd go outside!'

The parson said grace. I ignored him. I picked up my chicken in my right hand, my left hand being out of order, and suddenly felt Bob's spirit within me. I ate the chicken in a bestial manner (as he sometimes did) and stretched right across the table to dip it in the sauce before eating it and wiped my mouth on the back of my hand.

'I must say I don't think much of your table manners, young lady,' said the parson who suddenly looked as if he had AIDS.

'How the hell do you think St John the Baptist ate his chicken in the wilderness?' I shouted.

Miraculously, that achieved the result I wanted. The parson left in disgust.

* * *

Private Eye produced a cruel and evil cover the week after Bob died. It showed a close-up of his burial on the Mount of Olives. One pall-bearer had a caption coming out of his mouth saying 'Here Lies Robert

Maxwell.' The next pall-bearer had another caption which said 'He lied everywhere;' another said 'All 20 stone of him.' A caption from the body read 'You're All Fired.' The other captions were even worse.

I suggested to my personal doctor and dear friend, Victor Ratner*, that we should turn up at the offices of *Private Eye* unannounced and descend on Ian Hislop, the magazine's owner. Bob had always called him 'Pigslop' and his former partner Richard Ingrams, 'Mr Wigwam.'

Ratty felt as strongly as I did about the cover. He too was a friend of Bob's so he came willingly and without argument.

The offices of *Private Eye* were filthy. They looked like the contents of a Third World shack. In the front office, was a secretary/receptionist manning an old sixties switchboard. The walls were peppered from top to bottom with photographs of staff parties with Hislop occupying the limelight. In the fridge, which I was invited to open, was a jar of apple juice with a floating fungus on top.

The secretary was pleasant and sympathetic when Ratty and I walked in saying we wanted to speak to Hislop on urgent business. He called himself William Cartright and I called myself Natalie Klein.**

'Do, please take a seat,' said the secretary.' The only seat available was a sofa, which had seen better days, with a large hole in the middle from which springs could easily cut through one's clothing and scratch one's behind. A massive pile of old issues of the magazine, with coffee stains and cigarette burns on them, almost reached the ceiling. Half drunk cups of coffee lay on chipped occasional tables and on the floor.

'May I ask what you would like to discuss with Mr Hislop?' asked the secretary.

I was waiting for this.

'Yes,' I said. 'I was a cleaner on the *Ghislaine* on Maxwell's last journey. I know exactly how he died and he didn't fall accidentally, nor did he deliberately take his life, nor was he pushed. There was another woman with me,' I added vaguely.

The secretary took a gulp of coffee.

'Perhaps it would be much more appropriate to pull the Maxwell team straight away, rather than disturb Mr Hislop who's got to go to a funeral this afternoon.'

I was intrigued by the bizarre expression 'pull the Maxwell team'. Consultants use a similar phrase in hospital casualty departments. If a patient's heart stops beating, they say, 'Pull the crash team.'

* Dr Ratner tragically choked to death since I completed this book.
** Natalie Klein: The heroine of '*Never Alone with Rex Malone*' and the author's alter ego.

'What does "pull the Maxwell team" mean?' I asked, aghast.

'It means — send for the Maxwellologists.'

'Maxwellologists? Are they people who have graduated in Maxwellollogy?'

The woman showed no reaction; she finished her coffee and said 'They are the only people who can help you.'

'No, I want to see Mr Hislop personally. Besides, it is more likely than not that these people are out at lunch. Mr Cartwright and I are more than anxious to speak to Mr Hislop ourselves.'

Ratty was sitting on the damaged sofa reading a book describing the history of *Private Eye*.

'A fine binding,' he remarked, smiling at the secretary.

'Yes isn't it? I'll try Mr Hislop's line again.' This time, it rang. Hislop answered the phone.

'You can both go up now. The only thing is — you'll have to keep it brief, otherwise he'll miss his funeral.'

I struggled to keep a straight face. I was quite calm because I had swallowed a Valium half an hour before. Ratty went up the stairs first. As I followed him, I noticed the banister was so loose it was about to fall off.

We went into Hislop's office, each carrying our own copy of *Private Eye*. The office was just as dirty as the secretary's office. Hislop was far shorter than I had anticipated. He looked dishevelled and his office was saturated with an extremely unpleasant smell, a cross between truffles and leaking gas.

'So you're Natalie Cartwright?' he said.

'Natalie Klein. This is William Cartwright. Am I allowed to smoke a cigarette?'

'Yes,' said Hislop. It was clear that he was already extremely nervous although he did not know what was coming to him.

Ratty and I both sat down on two chairs, their linings torn, their springs sticking out and their covers frayed.

'I understand you were on Maxwell's boat the night he drowned and that you can tell me something about it,' said Hislop.

I looked at him, mimicking the serene smile of Miss Jean Brodie.

'It is true I have come to speak to you about something related to the Maxwell case.'

Before the little man had a chance to throw us out, I passed him the copy of *Private Eye* showing the offending cover. I leant over his desk and looked him straight in the eye.

113

'Have you ever lost anyone you loved, Mr Hislop?'

He looked as if a gun were being pointed at him and because of his short height, revealing only the top half of his head when he sat down, his appearance, in the case of a man who had upset so many unfortunates, was comical.

'Yes,' he eventually managed to splutter.

'I see. Would you care to see a picture like this displayed on the cover of a publicly-circulated magazine in relation to the person you lost?'

'No,' he murmured in an even more subdued voice.

'Mr Hislop, you suck and your rag sucks,' I said quietly.

I had already come to the conclusion that this tiny little man was a singularly poor conversational combatant. I wondered how on earth he managed to run a satirical magazine.

'Do you think there's a possibility that other people, and I refer in particular to Mrs Maxwell and her children, might be similar to you, in that they too might have feelings and be severely hurt by your behaviour?'

'I'm a professional man and it is inevitable that the people described in the *Eye* might sometimes get hurt. You know how I feel about Robert Maxwell.'

'Had you ever met Robert Maxwell?'

'No.'

'Why do you hold hostile feelings towards him if you never met him?'

'Because of all the harm he did.'

'Are you unaware of the extraordinary harm you yourself have done over the years with your pen, by ruining the lives and careers of innocent and decent people who have never hurt you, and who can't afford to sue you?'

The man Bob referred to as 'Pigslop' failed to answer. For some reason, he went very green, sweated copiously and started to shake. My one fear, namely of illness, surged through me. I was terrified he had flu.

'Have you got 'flu?' I shouted, petrified.

'No,' he murmured, inaudibly.

'I'll keep this discussion brief because I have other things to do, and so has William, but I won't leave until I've told you exactly what I think of you.'

Hislop slumped into the foul-smelling lining of his chair. By this time, I had completely lost my temper.

'You are a depraved little bastard. You spend all your time using your magazine to hurt people who have done nothing to provoke you.'

As I spoke, I could only see his forehead. He was staring straight into space like someone waiting for a train. I began to wonder whether he was all there. I continued, still shouting:

'You are even more inferior than the foulest order of louse-infested rent-boy except that the pus that seeps from your anus is not enough to equal the sick and sordid vitriol coming from the AIDS-ridden cock you call your pen!'*

I really couldn't make this man out. He just sat there like an owl waiting to be fed. There was a silence of about five minutes which he eventually broke. Up to now, I thought an aggrieved reader of his magazine had dragged him away somewhere and cut out his tongue. He turned to Ratty who had stared menacingly at him throughout the discussion without speaking. Hislop actually shouted: 'You! You! Why are you sitting in my office?'

Suddenly, it seemed the tension had been broken. I had to stand up and turn my back to Hislop. I had nervous hysterical giggles because of the way he was addressing Ratty.

'I am a friend of Miss Klein,' said Ratty. 'I happened to be lunching with her near by so I came in with her. I am also a doctor, so my other reason for coming is to apply First Aid in case she wishes to injure you.'

'Would you please take her outside,' said Hislop.

'Why? Is she doing anything illegal?'

'She's upsetting me. I told you to take her out.'

I moved towards the door in order to avoid an undignified scene. On Hislop's desk, on yellow paper, was a handwritten paragraph displaying a public school italic hand. I assumed it was the start of an attack on some other poor innocent. I went over and put my cigarette out on it.

'So, Mr Hislop, do you intend to apologize to Mrs Maxwell for this repellant and heinous outrage?' I asked as I walked towards the door.

'No,' he said bitterly.

'In that case, I'm afraid I shall have to put a curse on you if you don't apologize. You will lose someone else you love very, very soon. Also, I thought I'd remind you: Your offices smell of decomposing bodies. Can't you afford a cleaner or have you had too many writs?

He was obviously superstitious. He went as white as freshly-driven snow on the Steppes of Mother Russia and said nothing. Ratty and I left the building and went to a nearby pub.

'Well, what do you think Hislop did after we left?'

---

* I am obliged to remind the reader that the words in the last paragraph are purely metaphorical.

'I should think he threw up!' said Ratty.

Added to all this disciplinary energy expenditure was another incident in which I was obliged to become involved to defend the honour of the Maxwell family.

A woman called Nella Jones, who had set herself up as a spiritualist, wrote a grossly unpleasant and interminable article in the *Sun* about a conversation she was alleged to have had with Bob from beyond the grave. Throughout, she stressed that he appeared 'chilling' and 'evil'. She made the mistake of allowing the paper to print her picture above the article and foolishly allowed the rag to print the name of the town in which she lived, enabling me to find her telephone number.

I rang her up at midnight, a time which I assumed was inconvenient for her.

'Are you Nella Jones?' I shouted like a colonel.

A sleepy voice answered, 'Yes,' which reassured me I had disturbed her sleep.

'How much did the *Sun* newspaper pay you for that utterly disgraceful article you wrote in it today?'

'That's none of your fucking business! Leave me alone!'

Was this fear?

I pressed on.

'Do you know what they did to witches in the seventeenth century?'

'No.' (Why on earth didn't she hang up? Was she intrigued by any chance?)

'I'll tell you what they did to witches in the seventeenth century. They burned them alive,' I shouted.

'In the first place, this is the twentieth century. Secondly, I am not a witch; I am a spiritualist.'

'Do the two not come from the same family? You also know perfectly well that the dead do not have the power to speak to the living and the living do not have the power to speak to the bloody dead! How dare you call a dead man a crook when a British law court never even found him guilty! I bet you screwed a bomb out of that filthy rag.'

'Maxwell *was* a crook.'

'Oh? In the light of what I've just told you, you're not, I suppose?'

'Who the hell are you anyway?' she said.

'I only spill my name to people I respect and that certainly doesn't include a charlatan from the provinces who gets money playing on your clients' superstitions and then calls someone else a crook.'

The Jones woman was really taking off and so was I. It was like the famous fencing scene from the film *Theatre of Blood*.

'Are you a man or a woman?' she yelled. 'I can't tell with a voice like that.'

'A woman. Luckily I'm safely distanced from you, you batty old lesbian.'*

'Why do you think I'm that?'

'Because you don't know an attractive man when you see one.'

The woman gave me a smattering of Bob's physical and psychological faults and I returned her fire with a barrage of repulsive language and highly insulting personal remarks.

'By the way, how old are you?' She asked. 'You sound like a sex change of about 80.'

I ignored this and returned to her article in the *Sun* which has had a deeply upsetting effect on the entire Maxwell family.

'You don't think I'm for real, do you?' I shouted. 'I'll give you one warning and one warning only. I know exactly where you live. If you upset any member of the Maxwell family one more time, I will come to your house and throw sulphuric acid and in your face!'

I love a good blockbuster, particularly in Bob's honour, whether it be with a seemingly intelligent man of letters or a wench using the coarse language of the gutter.

One would think that circumstances would improve as the weeks passed following a loss. In fact I was able to tolerate the first few weeks quite well, occupying myself by seeing my friends, writing and blasting down phones at journalists. My arm was still out of order so I was not allowed to return to my office.

Because of the libel laws, I will not give the name of the Consultant who wilfully harmed me, for whom I was working, the department I was working in or indeed the name of the hospital. The prospect of beefy bailiffs knocking me up at dawn with writs in their hands is a daunting one. I will therefore refer to the consultant throughout as 'Dr Beria.'

Before I heard of Bob's death, when I was accounted for by witnesses as being in a very 'disturbed' state, Dr Beria had shown signs of being overtly in love with me without actually making physical passes at me. I had been working for him for 5 years and because he was particularly nice to me, in complimenting me coyly on my appearance and my efficiency, I liked him in return and stayed overtime every night to complete the large workload.

* This word is used metaphorically as the author is not familiar with Nella Jones's sexual proclivities.

As he returned to his office and saw me working overtime he would say 'Oh, bless you, love!' He always addressed women as 'love' when trying to chat them up which shows how inordinately common he was.

Dr Beria was of humble origins. He was born and bred in a provincial northern town and was a highly-spoilt only child. His mother, now a very old lady in an old peoples' home, had pursued a career, singing and dancing in clubs. I have heard, but only through rumour, that she earned her keep by an even less salubrious means and that Dr Beria's natural father was one of his mother's clients.

He fancied himself as a ladies man which, because of his physical appearance, was somewhat inappropriate. He was approximately 5 feet 8 inches tall and walked around in Hush-Puppies so that he could creep up behind his staff to make sure they were working.

From the front, his face looked like that of a weather-beaten old bulldog and his skin was reddish in areas as if he had impetigo. A pair of hideously unfashionable glasses was jammed on to his face, making his looks even more unprepossessing but, astonishingly to his credit, he had a pair of large blue eyes which gave a false impression of sensitivity.

In profile, he looked a bit better than frontways on. His appearance from the side conveyed a certain amount of masculinity and his nose though it looked as if it had been damaged in many a street brawl or boxing ring, still maintained a modicum of manliness in that it was vaguely aquiline in shape.

Mrs Beria, his mother, spent much of his childhood working, using the name Bethelemine Carmichael (name invented to avoid writs) and as he had no father to discipline him, his spoilt streak, perpetual desire to be pampered and his pathetic yearning for attention must have manifested themselves in him before he could walk.

Dr Beria loved his mother very much but must have been pretty petulant when she had to leave him to go to work. I imagine he threw vicious tantrums and may even have dragged the tablecloth from the table with everything on it as he saw her put on her hat to go out. It is known by psychologists that when only children become adults, they assume that they are sent by Providence to delight and be pampered by the opposite sex and to be regarded as being more important than anybody else in the world.

Such a specimen was Dr Beria. It was a blow to my vanity that I was not intuitive enough to recognize his two-faced personality, his spite in manipulating his staff behind their backs, his oily, artificial charm, his cowardice, caddishness and frequent rudeness, directed particularly at timid young nurses who feared him, and in particular at Irish women. He used to call the fiery Noreen Creedon 'Noraid' until one day she knocked him sideways with her awesome temper and he was polite to her ever since.

I was told by almost everyone in the department that Dr Beria was for some reason 'absolutely terrified' of me as well as being 'sexually attracted' to me to the point of being 'in pain.' The work I turned out for him was excellent and he used to leave little notes on my keyboard saying 'super work, love — very well done!'

My weakness (thank God Bob never knew or his high regard for me would have diminished) is that I am foolish enough to succumb to false flattery. This drug, almost worse than heroin, causes me to like the flatterer and to be blind to his reputation. I only keep company with those who flatter me and I sometimes shun and hurt loving friends who offer me distasteful advice for my own benefit. It is because of this weakness that I have made many needless enemies throughout my life although I have a large number of dear and loyal friends whose kindness I have always cherished and rewarded. I confess to being a vain, obsessive, vindictive and unforgiving enemy.

My first meeting with Dr Beria was unusual. I had been sent to work in another hospital that Monday morning and had been turned away because I had been double-booked. I then had orders to go straight to Dr Beria's hospital and report to him personally. I went to the manager of his office, out of breath and in a bad temper.

'I've had a terrible morning,' I said, my voice raised. 'I demand to see Dr Beria.' I no longer cared whether I'd be sent away or not. My spirits were low although *Never Alone with Rex Malone* had just been published but I was exhausted from lack of sleep.

I happened to notice a strange-looking man slumped in a swivel chair, doing absolutely nothing. I assumed he was a patient with a terminal illness.

'Where is Dr Beria?' I demanded.

The figure struggled to sit up straight. He looked somewhere in his 50s.

'I am Dr Beria,' he said in a breathy quiet, classless voice. 'Aren't you making rather a lot of noise?'

I shook his hand, apologized, introduced myself and agreed to be taken to my office. It was a nice, homely, little attic room with natural light blazing in through a huge window.

Two weeks had passed. I had done a big job for Dr Beria and because

I wanted to stay there I made sure I did it well, checking it repeatedly. I left it on his desk together with some new pens, pencils and rubbers, which I noticed he had a poor supply of. I took his empty coffee cup from his desk, tidied his papers, locked his office door behind me, as ordered, and got on with my other work.

The next day, Dr Beria came to his office to check his work. Then he rang me and asked me to go and see him. I assumed he was going to tell me that I was too slow so I made sure I was on my best behaviour. I knocked on the door of his office and he called me in.

'You wanted to see me, Dr Beria?' I said formally.

He raised some papers in front of me.

'Yes. Please sit down. Is this your work?'

'Yes, Dr Beria. Is it not all right?'

'It's not a question of it not being all right. It's absolutely superb.'

He was smiling. Half his teeth were missing. I smiled back. I confess to having developed some affection for him.

'Thank you, Dr Beria.'

I happened to be wearing white denim trousers and a blue and white striped T-shirt.

'Oh, love don't you look swish!'

'Indeed? Why do you say that?'

'You've got your sailor suit on again, I see and I love blonde women who are so efficient like you. Superb! Superb!'

'Thank you, Dr Beria,' I said like a butler. I did not fancy him and became embarrassed.

'You will have to excuse me now, Dr Beria.' I must go back to my office because I have to get on with my work.'

I walked towards the door, flattered but confused. Dr Beria half raised himself from his chair.

'I hope you will be staying with us for a long time,' he said. (I noticed his pronunciation of 'us' as 'uzz', the only verbal betrayal of his Northern origins.)

'I sincerely hope so, Dr Beria. After all, the devil you know is better than the devil you don't.'

Dr Beria looked at me with an almost demented expression on his face and his eyes began to fill with tears. By this time, I was mortified with embarrassment.

'Oh, love, you're not a devil!' he breathed. He sounded like a male version of Marilyn Monroe. I thought I was going to be sick.

'You must excuse me now, Dr Beria, my telephone is ringing and it could be for you.'

At 9.00 every morning I shared the lift with Dr Beria. Our offices were on the top floor. The lift was slow but, because I found it too strenuous to mount three flights of stairs, I had to go up with Dr Beria. Each morning the conversation between us was roughly the same.

'Oh, love, don't you look swish?'

Although Bob's origins were far humbler than Dr Beria's and his suffering more tortuous, Bob would never have been common enough to use words like 'love' or 'swish'. He would have been more likely to say 'smashing' because he never aspired to belong to a more sociologically exalted social rank than his position at birth.

Dr Beria, on the other hand, posed as an educated aristocrat, causing junior doctors to snigger into their hands and other consultants to ridicule him behind his back. Nurses hated him because of his sarcasm and secretaries hated him because of his rudeness. I was exempt from these discourtesies and had a great affection for him because he liked my work and looks and always showered me with false flattery which, in my naivety, I revelled in.

It was my third week working for Dr Beria. We were coming up in the slow, graffiti spattered lift. There were several messages on the walls saying things like 'Beria's an arsehole' which he ignored and stared at the floor.

There were two nurses in the lift besides Dr Beria and myself, talking about knitting patterns in South London accents. Neither was pretty and their faces were unpainted.

'Good morning, Dr Beria,' they both said cheerfully.

Dr Beria ignored their greeting and turned to me.

'What's your surname, Eleanor?' he asked with extreme courtesy.

'Berry.'

His voice became even more obsequious and I was sure he knew the answer to his next question before he asked it.

'I take it your family are the Berrys who used to own the *Telegraph?*' Although he asked affably enough, I was not liking the conversation and shifted from one foot to another.

'Yes. That's right,' I said abruptly. 'They've still got shares in the paper, though. How do you know all this about my family?'

'I only have to read about it in the *Sunday Times*. I'm not prying or anything,' he said apologetically.

'I don't take the *Sunday Times*,' I said coldly, 'or indeed any other of Rupert Murdoch's rags.'

For no apparent reason, Dr Beria suddenly gave his familiar look of a man who had just had his face slapped. I couldn't understand why he looked so upset. Maybe it was the abrupt tone of my voice.

'It's a cold day. I'll soon have a nice cup of coffee ready for you, Dr Beria,' I said sweetly. After all, I wanted to stay in my job.

We got out. The two nurses fixed me with a sneering grimace which I returned. This was not my first impression of ill-feeling within Dr Beria's department.

I shared the little office with a raunchy young girl called Debbie (surname withheld). She always wore a white blouse and a tight split skirt showing her flesh up to the thigh. She wore neither knickers nor tights and had on high-heeled black patent shoes. Her hair was thick, dark and curly like a gypsy's. Her voice was very girlish and her accent down-town Croydon. She and I had in common a love for Russian literature and Russian folk-songs which we discussed during breaks.

Dr Beria did not take long to notice Debbie's down-town Croydon accent which made him feel he could talk down to her although he used to ogle her bare legs as she walked down the corridor and her white blouse which descended into her cleavage, showing her lily-white skin.

Dr Beria was never rude to her when I was in the office because he was too much of a coward.

When I came back from lunch, I found Debbie rather subdued and red-eyed.

'What's wrong, Deb?'

'Dr Beria came in and shouted at me when you were out.'

'Why?'

'He just rushed in and said:- 'Give me three sharpened pencils and a clean rubber! That means immediately if you wish to stay here! '

Debbie had stared at him aghast.

'Well don't just sit there staring with your mouth gaping open like a cretin's! You're not deaf, are you?' He had apparently bellowed.

Debbie was composed.

'I will not be spoken to like that. I'm walking straight out of here.'

She walked calmly to the door and put on a neat, tailored white raincoat and picked up her bag and umbrella before her exit.

Dr Beria ran after her shouting like a madman. His white coat flapped behind him. It was too small for him and made him look ridiculous. He chased her as far as the tube station.

'I'm so sorry, Debbie, I get these funny turns sometimes. Oh, love, don't be upset. Please come back!'

Debbie was heavily overdrawn. She returned.

Debbie was also sex mad. She was fornicating several times a day with a junior doctor on Dr Beria's firm. The young doctor was by no means unique in hating Dr Beria who patronized him in front of patients on ward rounds. He and Debbie found fornicating ground in the hospital hard to locate, but locate it they did, for such was their overwhelming lust.

In the mornings, they used Dr Beria's lavatory and although they found that the bizarre consultant sometimes forgot to pull the chain, they were undeterred and reached screaming climaxes which were mercifully unheard except by me.

A few hours later, they used a telephone box just outside the mortuary and were said by passers-by, working in the hospital, to be making enough noise to wake the dead.

It was when they chose Dr Beria's desk when he was supposed to be in Harley Street that they got into serious trouble. Dr Beria's two private patients had cancelled so he had come back prematurely.

'There is a time and a place for everything,' he said mildly. 'I feel this is letting down the firm.'

Debbie was sacked. Dr Beria didn't have the guts to sack her himself and asked the Administrator to do so on his behalf.

It did not take long for 5 years to pass by. A lot of staff members resented the fact that Dr Beria favoured me above all the others and that I was introduced by him to the Mayor when he said my services were invaluable to the department, and better than those of any other member of his staff.

Sometimes when I was alone in the office, he would come in and throw all the air in his lungs into a breathless, galumphing, Natasha-esque* 'Hi,' dragging his lips apart from ear to ear in a maniacal grimace, desperately intended to be a smile.

The people at the receiving end of his sarcasm and rudeness began to dislike and deeply resent his courtesan behaviour towards me. He was always offering to carry things for me. Sometimes, he would say, 'You're a real star!' in front of the people he patronized. His obvious unrequited love for me embarrassed me and caused my colleagues to dislike me even more. But because this plain, pathetic man was always so affectionate towards me, it was hard for me not to be fond of him. In a way I felt like the Victorian actress Madge Kendal when she was with the Elephant Man.

* Natasha: Heroine of *War and Peace* (Tolstoy) — Lively, vivacious and innocent when a child.

123

One morning, I brought him his coffee. He looked pretty odd, but not much odder than usual. He was talking down two telephones at once. I could tell that his wife was at the receiving end of the telephone in his right hand, and that his mistress was on the left hand line. His voice became gruff as he shielded the mouthpiece of the left-hand phone.

'I won't be back before 1.00 in the morning. Put my dinner in the microwave and open a bottle of claret. No, I can't get back earlier, I'm too busy!'

He hung up without saying 'goodbye' and spoke into the left-hand phone.

'Oh, love, my dearest, dearest love. You asked who I was speaking to. It was only the wife! It's been too long, oh so very long. If I don't see you tonight, I'll die.'

The voice at the other end must have consented.

'Oh, I'm so happy! Oh, my dear little turtle dove, my love, my love!'

I strongly regretted not having taken a sick bowl into Dr Beria's office.

I began to receive hate mail from within the hospital but my determination to find out who sent it, killed my irritation.

An anonymous female caller with a South London accent rang me up. She had rung several times before.

'There's a parcel for you at the gatehouse,' she said. 'I'd like to see you wearing a pair of crotchless rubber knickers.'

I collected a large brown envelope. It was addressed to 'The Boss's little darling.' Intrigued, I ripped the envelope open. In it was an empty Coca-Cola bottle, a handkerchief smothered with dark pink lipstick, some loose salted nuts and a used tampon.

I showed all this stuff to Dr Beria who was baffled but not irritated.

'Next time the woman calls, put her straight on to me.' I told him she had rung before and (truthfully) that she would be unlikely to make these calls to men, only women, so if he was going to answer, he would have to put on a woman's voice.

'I can have a jolly good try!' he said, raising his voice two octaves. I thought this was rather witty and charming and laughed.

'Let me make you a coffee for a change, love,' he said.

* * *

All this took place towards the end of October 1991. I got on with my work and he continued to leave me affectionate notes to say how well it was done. The words 'Oh love, you really are a star!' were never off his lips.

His love for me was claustrophobic, particularly as I did not find him attractive. I continued to work overtime and to see that his work was done to perfection. I loved the hospital and was supremely happy there. I revelled in the opportunity to gossip with other women outside my department and, as we walked round the square smoking and eating cake during breaks, we talked and cackled like a load of ribald washerwomen.

I had no idea that my happiness was soon to be destroyed and my life ruined by a bitchy, spiteful little man in the form of Dr Beria who discovered that another man, and not he, was the object of my adulation and hero-worship. I also had no idea that this doctor, whose function was to relieve pain rather than to inflict it, could change from Jekyll to Hyde overnight and sadistically kick a bereaved woman as she lay bleeding in the gutter.

Dr Beria was invariably unkind and vicious when thwarted. Perhaps he was unaware of his unprepossessing appearance. His behaviour towards me when Bob was drowned and when he became aware of our close friendship, was one of the cruellest episodes of conduct I have ever personally witnessed in my life. Were he to stand next in line with the original Lavrenti Beria from whom I have deliberately taken his name, the outrageously merciless head of Stalin's Secret Police, would have appeared like the owner of a home for birds with broken wings in comparison.

It was Ratty who first informed me of Dr Beria's snide attitude towards my accident and my grief. A month before, he had told Ratty I was the best worker in his department.

Ratty rang him up the next morning to say that I would have to be off work for a few weeks because of the accident and the fact that I could not use my arm until the plaster was off.

'Well of course, in view of what's just happened, we all expected this,' he said, apparently very unpleasantly. 'She was exceptionally disturbed when she heard the news, not at all unlike a mental patient. At any rate, that's what I heard.'

Ratty was disgusted.

'I think that's a pretty obnoxious way to talk, considering her loyalty to you, how hard she has always worked for you, sometimes staying over until 8.00 to complete the work. Besides, you told me she was your best worker as well as telling the Mayor.'

There was a pause. Dr Beria could dish out sarcasm to timid, unintelligent underlings, but words came slowly to him when he was cornered by his equals in rank.

'That was then. This is now,' he eventually muttered, adding: 'You do know she's been crossed off the books of most employment agencies, don't you?' This was an evil, vicious slanderous lie.

On all occasions in the past when I had returned to work after leave, Dr Beria made a point of giving the impression that he had been crossing off the days waiting for me. As soon as I came back to the office, he would kiss me on both cheeks and say, 'Ever so nice to have you back, love!'

I returned after Christmas. The plaster had been taken off my arm but my left hand was still swollen. The only person who seemed pleased to see me was the Administrator who was also a nurse and who kept asking me to show her my arm. I automatically extended my right arm, every time she asked. I thought she wouldn't be able to tell the difference between left and right immediately. She didn't fall for this, however, and insisted on seeing the other arm which she said was still not fit for use. She put me on switchboard duties which I have always enjoyed and which helped me to relax a bit.

Apart from the kind-hearted Administrator, many of the staff in the department were cold and hostile towards me, despite my friendly overtures. Noreen Creedon said she could have done without my relatives ringing me up just after the drowning. She also ticked me off for drinking alcohol after a shock. I could have done without that but didn't open combat with her then because I was feeling too weak.

The atmosphere in the main office downstairs where the switchboards were, was cold and unwelcoming but I befriended two newcomers called Mark and Justine with whom I was able to share jokes and I was always on friendly terms with Margaret Samuels, the Appointments Manager.

The morning I first saw Dr Beria again, I was made to feel so miserable that I thought of resigning.

He came over to where I was sitting. He didn't say 'hello,' ask me how I was or indeed say he was pleased to see me.

'Ring this number and get my son on his bleep,' he commanded.

I did as I was told but his son's switchboard didn't answer. Dr Beria went outside because he was too impatient to stand waiting, and returned in 5 minutes.

'Come on, haven't you found my son yet?'

'No, because his switchboard hasn't answered yet,' I said coldly.

'Let me do it for you,' he said. 'I expect I'll get him more quickly than you can.'

'Oh, please do!' (with extreme sarcasm and a fishwife's grimace, raising my upper lip, showing only my top front teeth). I don't think the bastard even noticed.

I rushed upstairs to Noreen's office nearly in tears. How could these people be so hostile towards me when I had done nothing wrong!

'Help me, Noreen. We're still friends, damn it! Why are all these people downstairs deliberately making me so unhappy?'

Noreen stopped working and turned to me without smiling.

'Because they're sorry for those poor *Mirror* pensioners, I should imagine. Aren't you?'

I've always felt sorry for the terrible injuries inflicted on Londoners by those bloody fellow countrymen of yours but at least I've never thrown it in your face up to now because I've got decent manners! At least when my father dies he won't be buried with the Sinn Fein flag draped over his coffin.'

I rushed out slamming the door, feeling like a South African black on a whites only train. I was hurt and wretched and went to the Administrator in tears. My intention was to have Noreen Creedon relieved of her responsibilities.

The Administrator was pleasant and sympathetic. I told her what was wrong and also how hurt I was on reading the papers every day and finding nothing but evil about Bob who had never been tried in a British court of law.

'Go on home,' she said. 'I'll speak to Dr Beria. I don't think you're fit to work the switchboard today.'

'I'm paid to work from 9.00 to 5.00,' I said. 'I'm not ill. I'll be OK in a minute.'

She gave me some tea.

'This will help. I know just how you feel. Why don't you go outside and get some nicotine into your lungs? Then come back and we'll have a talk.'

I returned in an even more paranoid state.

'I know there's a mass movement here to persecute me and throw me out. This hospital is my second home and the people who work in it are my second family.'

I was touched by her kindness.

'You're talking like this because you're not well. No-one's trying to get rid of you. Besides, you're a very good worker. You must go home now and come back in the morning. Have a nice long sleep and you'll be an entirely different person.'

I returned the next day and sat down by the two switchboards. Very few calls were coming in that morning. I got out the thriller by James Hadley Chase I had brought with me and its compulsive, gripping pace took my mind off my misery.

Dr Beria came over to me.

'Oh, James Hadley Chase,' he said. 'My favourite book of his is *No Orchids for Miss Blandish*. Since he died, a lot of other books have been ghosted in his name — at least, that's what I've heard.'

I could tell he was making an overt effort to be friendly but his manner was artificial as if the Administrator had had a word with him.

'Someone said Kingsley Amis ghosts his books,' I said politely.

Dr Beria turned off the charm it had been such a strain to muster. He just walked out of the room.

When my arm was better, I was moved back into the office I shared with Noreen, the office in which I heard about Bob's death.

The sun was beaming in which cheered me greatly and I felt my troubles were behind me.

'I'm sorry about what I said the other day,' said Noreen.

'So am I.'

'I really didn't mean to hurt you. It just came out.'

I cleaned my screen by spitting on it and wiping it with a cloth. I turned the machine on and got it ready.

'OK, OK,' I said. 'It's all right as long as you don't ever do it again.'

'I just don't understand why you went over the top like that. Maxwell wasn't even related to you.'

'I don't want to hear any more from you about Robert Maxwell and I really do mean that,' I said quietly. 'I've got a lot of work to do and I must get on with it.'

Two weeks passed by. I had become on fairly good terms with Noreen and she, Doris and I used to go drinking after office hours. Doris had formerly worked for Dr Beria but found him so repulsive that she went to work for a consultant Geriatrician in the hospital who was civil and appreciative of her hard work.

Once I had settled down, I became a new person. I got on with Dr Beria's work and made sure it was done to perfection so that he couldn't complain. I visited all my friends in the hospital and gossiped as before.

Dr Beria continued to ignore me. If he wanted to leave something in the office for me to do, he always did so, having made sure I was out of the room so that he wouldn't have to speak to me. My disdain for him increased but, as long as I did his work perfectly, I thought there was nothing he could do to hurt me.

My wellbeing was short-lived.

It was 11.30 a.m. on Friday 14 February 1992, St Valentine's Day. Dr Beria came quietly towards me, giving me one of his false and almost toothless smiles.

'May I have a word in my office, love?'

I said nothing but did as I was told. I went straight in. I had no idea what was happening, only the knowledge that Dr Beria was obsessed by Robert Maxwell and as he was Head of the Directorate, I would have to put up a heroic fight to win.

The Head of Personnel, a tiny little woman in glasses from Liverpool, sat in a chair immediately next to Dr Beria behind his desk. The seating arrangement was designed to terrify but I had Bob's spirit burning within me, and a gold locket with his photograph in it round my neck. I sat down opposite the ridiculous looking couple.

'So what's all this in aid of?' I asked confidently but not aggressively.

'I am worried about you, Eleanor,' said Dr Beria.

I looked at him defiantly.

'If you waste your time worrying about me, might I suggest that your other worries and problems must be somewhat remote?' The sneer in my voice was distinctly recognizable.

The woman spoke. She didn't half look odd.

'Dr Beria *likes* you!' she boomed in a thick Liverpool brogue.

'Why have you called me in here?' I asked quietly.

'Dr Beria's worried sick.'

I raised my eyes as if talking to a couple of nuts.

'Why?' My voice was almost a shout.

'Because he thinks you have a psychiatric illness,' said the tiny little woman.

'I didn't know he was a psychiatrist.'

'He thinks this because you don't relate to people in a normal manner.'

I took off my jacket and threw it on the floor.

'I'd appreciate it if you would generate this statement in a more palpable vernacular.'

'I don't understand what you said.'

'Christ! The woman didn't even understand English!

'I meant, back up your statement with evidence. I find this talk, which I suspect to be a rubbishy witch-hunt, a ludicrous waste of time. I have a lot of work to do and would appreciate it if you would let me get on with it.'

It seemed as if this extraordinary interrogation had been rehearsed beforehand. The words of the man and woman were stilted and unnatural. Occasionally they stopped mid-sentence as if they had forgotten their lines.

'You have a reputation in this hospital for being somewhat eccentric,' said the woman.

'OK, so I'm eccentric. Why shouldn't I be eccentric?' I said aggressively. 'I am an exceptionally hard and loyal worker. The fact that I'm eccentric is neither here nor there.'

'The British don't tolerate eccentricity,' she said.

'I *am* British!' I shouted.

After a long silence Dr Beria spoke.

'I believe you're very unhappy here. You are emotionally disturbed.'

I rose to my feet and leant over the desk, pointing my index finger at Dr Beria's face.

'Dr Beria, I have served you for 5 whole years with loyalty and dedication. You told someone I was the best you'd ever had and you said exactly the same thing to the Mayor. I have pandered to your requirements, such as making you coffee whenever you wanted it. I have worked overtime almost every evening to do your work to perfection.

'The answer is, yes, I am unhappy, I am unhappy because I am hurt. In the past you welcomed me back to work every time I had been on leave. "How are you? Nice to see you back? Are you better?" These words were forever on your lips.

'This time, all you did was command me to get hold of your son without so much as saying "please." '

I noticed his hangdog expression. He lowered his head so that his forehead was almost touching the desk. He blushed like a flighty debutante. I could even see tears in his eyes.

'But I've never actually been rude to you, have I?' he asked pathetically.

'Not half as rude as you are to timid Irish nurses who are too thick to answer you back, but rude enough.'

'When was I rude?'

'I can give you a flagrant example. I passed you in the corridor yesterday morning and said "good morning, Dr Beria". I didn't hear so much as a blessed murmur!'

'I didn't hear you. Otherwise I would have said "good morning".'

I remained standing and my voice grew louder.

'It's not only that, Dr Beria. You've been deliberately avoiding me.

Outside in the square, you turn and walk in the opposite direction when you see me. You leave your work in my office when you know I'm elsewhere. You deliberately shirk contact with me and make it obvious you don't want me here.'

Again, the haunted hangdog expression, the blush and the moist eyes.

'Eleanor, I called you because you are ill. I'm offering you two weeks' sick-leave.'

I wished with all my heart I'd taken it but I wanted to protect myself with an image of selfless industry.

'I'm not ill and I'm not taking two weeks' off!'

'You're ill in mind.'

'How the hell do you know?'

'Let's face it. Your reaction to Robert Maxwell's death was pretty abnormal.'

I lost my temper and the old oaf looked scared.

'What abnormality lies in human grief? You've no idea how much that man meant to me!'

'No normal person would grieve for a man like that,' said Dr Beria.

'Do you mean a greater and better-looking man than you?'

He repeated the hangdog stunt. These words must have upset him. Yes! He really was jealous of Bob. He wore exactly the same expression as he had when I had gone to his Harley Street rooms to discuss my impending return to the hospital.

'I understand you were very upset by Robert Maxwell's death,' he had said.

'Yes, I was and still am. He was such a lovely man and so attractive as well.'

He had stared at me as if he had been bitten in the testicles by a rat. It was then that his jealousy was confirmed in my mind.

Back in the hospital, he continued to vent his envy of Bob on me.

'When you were told that Robert Maxwell was dead, you asked one of the consultants to go out and buy you a bottle of whisky.'

'That's a filthy, bloody lie and you know it!' I screamed. 'Besides I never drink whisky.'

'I was told you started a fire that night.'

'Mindless ludicrous fabrication, Dr Beria, and you know it!'

'You did start a fire. The matter was reported. You nearly set the whole building on fire. You can't go round starting fires just because someone's fallen out of a boat.'

If I had had a weapon on me, I would have killed the bastard outright.

'Dr Beria, your sense of humour is disgusting and macabre,' I shrieked. 'I'll tolerate no more of this! You've tried to break my spirit but you have failed. By the time I've reported this vile outrage to the Board of Governors, you'll be ruined, Beria!'

Dr Beria faked calmness. 'I understand you actually tried to ring up the Queen.'

'Which Queen do you have in mind, Dr Beria?'

It is indeed true that I tried to ring up the Queen to complain about the repulsive joke about Bob's death that Prince Andrew made at the American Embassy.*

Beria finally looked as if he could take no more. He was like a bull about to die at the end of a fight.

'I've got to teach my students now,' he said to the personnel woman. 'Will you take over from me?'

'Don't worry. I'll be able to handle her.'

'I need a cigarette,' I said when Dr Beria had gone. 'May I smoke in here?' She said I could. Once I'd lit up, I felt more relaxed.

After Dr Beria had gone, the tiny little woman moved to another chair on my side of the desk.

'What exactly was the deceased to you?'

'Don't call him "the deceased". His name was Mr Maxwell. He was my hero, my idol and my friend and he still is all of those things.'

The woman looked as if I had come from another planet. I had to put my hands behind my back to stop myself hitting her.

'Did you have an affair with Robert Maxwell?' she asked, leaning forward in her chair like a ghoul ogling a circus freak.

Try as I did, I couldn't control my temper.

'That's none of your fucking business!' I bellowed but when I realized what I'd said, I felt I had to change the wording, if only to save my skin.

'Sorry, what I meant was, that's none of your accursed business,' I said in a calmer tone.

I had no idea what she wanted out of me and because of her towering rank, she was beginning to alarm me. She said nothing but stared straight at my eyes in a manner which gave me the creeps.

Nobody has ever stared me out in my life. Even on underground trains, I have forced myself to go to anything up to ten stations beyond my destination to outstare someone with the odious impertinence to ogle my eyes.

* The "joke" made by Prince Andrew at the American Embassy was of such inordinate obscenity that even I am incapable of writing it down.

Her eyes, peering into mine from behind her round glasses, were small, blue and piercing. I was determined not to avert my gaze. We stared at each other for at least 5 minutes until she finally backed down and broke into a smile which I graciously returned.

Perhaps I daunted her. Whatever the position was, she terminated the interview. We left Dr Beria's dingy office and went out into the corridor. Because I had shouted at her and used the F word, I felt obliged to compliment her by remarking on the 'beauties' of her home town and she responded with extreme courtesy and affability.

'Ah, yes, you recognized my accent, didn't you?'

'That's right. What's going to happen to me now?'

'You'll receive a letter or a phone call next week sometime, summoning you to a disciplinary hearing in the offices of Personnel.'

'So I'm to be disciplined because I loved Robert Maxwell, am I? More so than Dr Beria. This rather reminds me of Henry II turning on his once-beloved friend, Thomas à Becket for loving God more than him.'

Yet again, she looked at me as if I were incurably insane.

'Not having heard of either of these people, I can't respond to your remark,' she said.

Good God! Didn't this woman go to school?

She flounced off without saying 'goodbye' in her cheap, white, clattering stilettos.

I heard nothing further the next week. I assumed that it was not against hospital regulations to have loved Robert Maxwell and that nothing further was going to happen to me. All my friends, including my family, were convinced I was in the clear, but to cover myself, I consulted a solicitor as well as my father who offered to turn up at Dr Beria's Harley Street consulting rooms to challenge him if necessary.

A month later, my telephone rang. The caller was my Union representative from NALGO of which he was Branch Secretary.

'Dr Beria's complained that relations between him and you have irretrievably broken down and he wants you moved into another department.'

'For Christ's sake, the man's demented! Why?'

'Have you not heard the rumour?'

'I'll take a guess. Dr Beria's a closet queen and he wanted Maxwell himself.'

The union rep showed no sense of humour whatsoever.

'Listen carefully, and keep calm. A rumour has circulated round this hospital that you stormed on to a ward where you confronted a man who was dying of cancer. The man, wizened and hopelessly gasping for breath, was surrounded by his sobbing family while a priest was giving him the last rites.

'Apparently a complaint was made that you barged past the priest, roughly pushing him aside and that you leant over the dying man, barking: "Your time's up, Squire. We need the organs that haven't been hit! Come on, hurry up. You'll have to ask for a form and fill it in before you croak!" '

I was too shocked to shout.

'This story's a disgusting, bloody lie,' I muttered.

'I know that. We all know that. My advice to you is to get away from this doctor. He has the power to do anything he wants to you. He has status. You don't.'

Soon after, Dr Beria engineered a situation whereby I was moved to a department in which one person after another was being made redundant because of draconian cutbacks put in motion by John Major's Government. My redundancy soon came up, but as he would have wished, Dr Beria could not be legally charged with dismissing me since he had only transferred me.

By God, I shall punish him one day but I won't do so yet because it is still too close to the vile crime he committed towards a woman bleeding in the gutter.

I have been ill since I had to leave the hospital I loved. I now suffer from excessively low blood pressure for which there is no medication so I sleep most of the day. In addition, I had an echocardiogram which was abnormal and it was pointed out to me that this was caused by severe stress alone since there is no history of heart disease in my family.

It was explained to me that the abnormally fast speed of my heart was due to one of its valves being 'sluggish' and not pulling its weight. Hence the blood pumped by the heart is not getting to the brain fast enough, causing me migraines, starting behind the eyes and radiating to the bottom of the spine, giddiness, fainting attacks, palpitations and exhaustion. Sometimes I am kept awake at night by the little bugger crashing against my ribs.

I won't be able to get my own back on that bastard until I am well, but I will in the end as I believe in an eye for an eye and a tooth for a tooth. I hope with all my heart he reads this book and is caused as much pain as he has caused me.

Nobody in the world can call me a coward. Like F.E. Smith, my maternal grandfather, I can see no bad in a friend and no good in an enemy. Despite the cruelty I have suffered by the hands of evil, down-right nasty parties, and the distressing rumours in the Press, I have never failed to fight valiantly and unbetrayingly for Bob's honour, his glowing image in my mind and finally the honour of Betty, his widow.

My sad story has now come to an end and I am up to the present time — I have lost my dear friend, Ratty as well and at the moment I am jobless.

CONCLUSION

Robert Maxwell was not in any way like other mortals. His personality and conduct were utterly unique. His manner in relating to others was unusual. Spiritually, he stood apart from others; his right hand did not know what his left hand was doing and because of that no one, not even any member of his family, actually knew him entirely and I don't think he even knew himself.

When family life no longer afforded him the relief he sought from his black thoughts, he threw himself into projects quite pathologically just as a junkie, his psyche wrecked by hideous memories, turns to heroin. Bob identified most with *Don Giovanni* but it was not endless numbers of women he conquered but companies, newspapers, football clubs and anything else he could get hold of to call his.

There were elements in him which were distinctly Heathcliffian. He was sometimes capable of intimidating and boarish behaviour towards other men, particularly effete young men with little drive, who courted his daughters. What comes to mind particularly is the Italian who was keen on Ghislaine and who had had a bit of a battering. If such men happened to meet him when he was clouded by Slavic gloom, he tended to terrify them and they never returned to the house. Strangely he often said that I myself was terrifying!

On the other hand, his inordinate kindness and generosity seeking nothing in return, was unique, extraordinary and legendary.

He was savagely intolerant of fools and of anyone who couldn't make him laugh. His very definite sense of humour frequently lifted his Slavic glooms and he would become playful, jolly and as cheeky as a child.

He enjoyed horseplay, simple practical jokes, pinching women's behinds and deliberately annoying people by throwing rubbish out of car windows, throwing bathing-suited women into swimming pools and sometimes even clinging to their skirts.

He loved things of simple beauty such as ballet, the fragrance of flowers, the crispness of mountain snow, the chirping of small children and music which never appeared to bore him. He liked beautiful young women in brightly-coloured clothes with roses in their hair. He also liked girls who were cheeky, courageous, attractive and affectionate. Towards those he cherished, his love knew no boundaries.

Readers of this book may have gained the impression that I regarded Robert Maxwell as a saint. If they have then they have been misled but because of the generalized tenor of the book, it is not my intention to blame them.

He may have been my hero, idol and friend. I may have worshipped the ground he walked on but still I recognize that, like all other mortals, he was no saint.

He was a very lonely man and even the presence of his wife, family and friends sometimes failed to exorcize the demons within him. The horrific and barbaric murder of his family during the War cast a weighty and unlifting shadow upon him. No doubt his secret shame of having been afraid of his tyrannical father, contrasting with the Rambo image he showed to the world, haunted him as well. He often said he was going to write a book about loneliness one day.

Although devoted to his wife and family, I have never thought of him as being a happy man which could be an explanation for the most singular manner in which he related to his staff.

Contrary to superficial and indeed much exaggerated reports, there was not an ounce of cruelty in his being. He was honourable and fair and had a heart of gold, but because of the unusual nature of his voice, the amount of noise he made (probably without being aware of it), his sudden and overbearing demeanour and the sheer robustness of his build, added to his overpowering sexuality (concentrated sex oozed from every pore of his person when he wasn't too overweight), he had an ability to terrify people to shaking wrecks, a trait I myself picked up from him to use when I can't get my own way.

Since his death, terrible things have been said about him in the Press because the cowards who wrote about him knew he was no longer there to hit back. It would be an understatement to say that he was not the evil crook he was made out to be — certainly not to the extent his tabloid persecutors were, in order to make vast sums of money, having no regard for the deep psychological harm they did to his widow and children.

The media forgets that he only had two years' formal education and certainly no training in accountancy. It is known that the Board of Trade published a report, so called, in 1970, stating he was unfit to be at the stewardship of a publicly quoted company, owing to a cock-up regarding the sale of encyclopedias. Had he deliberately intended to deceive, why was he not arrested? Why was he not jailed? The answer is that there was no evidence that he was a fraud or a crook.

I do not profess to know anything about what I call 'haute finance' but any unbiased, fair-minded person would tell us that he made extremely hasty decisions in rare moments of euphoria and could be inappropriately cavalier in his judgement.

He told me once he was a schizophrenic and he may have been right. When he reverted to the child, Lajbi, and in many ways the Lajbi side of his personality prevailed over the Bob side, there were moments when he acted impulsively without sufficient regard of consequence.

Moreover, although he worked like a pit pony for almost 24 hours a day, resulting in his ingenious capacity for creating capital, much of which he channelled, among other things into a myriad of charities and other significant concerns, I don't think he had an entirely mature understanding of money once he had made it, what to use it for or where to put it. This is not an uncommon trait in individuals who have raised themselves unaided from dire poverty to riches.

The affair regarding the *Mirror* pensioners could be another example of the disorderly side of his personality and indeed of his rapidly-progressing terminal illness, dramatically hastened by the lethal sedative, Halcion, now removed from the market. Indeed, even his speech was distorted towards the end of his life, in that he referred to monkeys as minkeys. He had been on this drug for insomnia for decades at a colossal dosage.

On 29 May 1991, a document was signed apparently authorizing the transfer of over £400 million. It was not taken into account that Bob was totally immobilised for a year before his death. The emphysema in his remaining lung was so severe that he could hardly breathe. His brain was seriously deprived of oxygen. His thinking processes were diminished to the extent that he was almost a vegetable. His behaviour had become distinctly bizarre and some instances of this were so extreme that it would be grossly unkind to list them.

He was bedridden most of the time with an oxygen mask on his face. If he had been capable of holding a pen and signing any documents, he would not have known what he was writing on.

Others have different stories to tell but these are beyond my comprehension.

There is speculation as to whether some transfers were being made before his illness. He was like a juggler trying in desperation to keep about fifteen balls in the air at a time, in the heat of one of the darkest recessions this country has ever known.

Perhaps in a fit of cavalier optimism, when he again reverted to the child Lajbi, clinging to his mother's skirts, he assumed he could repay the missing money in better times.

He could not possibly have taken it without intending to return it and on top of that he was never even tried by a British court of law where you are innocent until you are proved guilty.

I have read the book that has recently come out by Nick Davies who is reputed to be confused about whether or not he had ever been to Ohio. The book is fascinating but shows a palpable disregard for truth. In it, Davies says Bob called him to his bedroom when he was in bed with a cold on a rainy Sunday afternoon. Davies says Bob was 'suicidally' depressed and wanted to 'jump out of the window and end it all'.

Half-witted readers, apparently unaware that the human mood is not static, regard this incident as evidence for his having deliberately ended his life. Balls! Most sufferers from bad colds become depressed, particularly on rainy Sunday afternoons and they don't end their lives.

Davies tells us of an implausible incident occurring in Paris, concerning an argument between Bob and Betty about an overcoat. Bob is accounted for as getting into a bait because she told him he would get a cold if he didn't button his overcoat up. Davies said Bob told her to 'f*** off'. He would never have spoken to her like that although he often got very bad tempered when she fussed over him or gave him any advice about his health. I asked Betty whether Bob had told her to 'f*** off' and she hotly denied it. She said that Bob very rarely used this word when addressing women anyway.

As for the allegation that his children virtually trembled at meals when he was present, I never noticed any such instances. On one occasion, for example, Christine's twin sister, Isabel said something across the table to her father about Turgenev (the Russian writer), pronouncing the name incorrectly.

Her father rounded on her, his mouth full of steak and ticked her off for not pronouncing the name right.

'Do you have to be so awful, Daddy?' Isabel retorted, piqued. 'I don't know anything about Russian literature, do I?'

Was this fear?

Bob told Ghislaine that her dress was indecent and Ghislaine picked up a bowl of strawberries and threatened to throw it over her father's head.

Was this fear?

Kevin, aged about 16, called across the table to his father: 'Is the Honourable Member for Buckingham, still capable of rising?'

(Damned impertinent, I thought.) Was this fear?

If the signs of the zodiac are to be believed, Bob was a Gemini. I believe he may have had a split personality and that Lajbi could have possibly shifted the funds without Bob knowing anything about it. But there again male Geminis are very strange creatures and all decent people should make allowances, particularly for terminally ill Geminis.

If it is of any relevance, Bob was a born again religionist who took his beliefs extremely seriously. Would such a man have knowingly ruined other people's lives? No. A hell of a lot of financiers on the *Daily Mirror* are corrupt and I suspect that they and not a man with an oxygen-deprived brain, who had been taking the lethal drug Halcion for decades, were guilty.